THE RISE OF THE KINGDOM WARRIOR

"Awakening the Church to Her Kingdom Assignment"

Prophet Joshua A. Cable

Love Clones Publishing
www.lcpublishing.net

Copyright © 2015 by Joshua A. Cable

All rights reserved. This book or any portion thereof may not be reproduced or used in any manner whatsoever without the express written permission of the publisher except for the use of brief quotations in a book review.

Printed in the **United States** of America

First Printing, 2015

ISBN: 978-0692438039

English Standard Version
Scripture quotations marked "ESV" are from the ESV Bible® (The Holy Bible, English Standard Version®), copyright © 2001 by Crossway Bibles, a publishing ministry of Good News Publishers. Used by permission. All rights reserved.
http://www.crossway.org

King James Version
Scripture quotations marked "KJV" are taken from the Holy Bible, King James Version (Public Domain).

New International Version
Scripture quotations marked (NIV) are taken from the Holy Bible, New International Version®, NIV®. Copyright © 1973, 1978, 1984 by Biblica, Inc.™ Used by permission of Zondervan. All rights reserved worldwide.
http://www.zondervan.com

New Living Translation
Scripture quotations marked (NLT) are taken from

the Holy Bible, New Living Translation, copyright ©
1996, 2004, 2007 by Tyndale House Foundation.
Used by permission of Tyndale House Publishers,
Inc., Carol Stream, Illinois 60188.
All rights reserved.
http://www.newlivingtranslation.com/
http://www.tyndale.com

The Living Bible
Copyright © 1971 by Tyndale House Foundation.
Used by permission of Tyndale House Publishers Inc.,
Carol Stream, Illinois 60188. All rights reserved. The
Living Bible, TLB, and The Living Bible logo are
registered trademarks of Tyndale House Publishers.

Holman Christian Standard Bible®
Copyright © 1999, 2000, 2002, 2003, 2009 by
Holman Bible Publishers.
Used with permission by Holman Bible Publishers,
Nashville, Tennessee. All rights reserved.

Contemporary English Version®
Copyright © 1995 American Bible Society. All rights
reserved.
Bible text from the Contemporary English Version
(CEV) is not to be reproduced in copies or otherwise
by any means except as permitted in writing by
American Bible Society, 1865 Broadway, New York,
NY 10023 (www.americanbible.org).

DEDICATION

This book is dedicated to every citizen of the Kingdom of God that is in need of a stirring in their hearts for end time revival.

ACKNOWLEDGEMENTS

I want to first thank my Heavenly Father for His grace to write this work for His people. The times spent receiving revelation for this book has been absolutely wonderful. God, I love you and look forward to more experiences writing in the Spirit. I want to also say thank you to my lovely and beautiful wife, Monica, for your prayers and critiques for this book. Honey, thank you for encouraging and pushing me to finish when I was up late at night half sleep. I love you much! I look forward to your published book that the world will experience.

I want to next thank my anointed auntie Pastor Jolinda Wade for your inspiration. Thank you for allowing my family and me to stay in your home when God led us to move to Chicago. When you were enduring the process of publishing your book (Divine Grace Behind the Walls) I was learning. I knew I would be writing a book and I watched you go through the dos and don'ts and it taught me. Without these next three people there would be no book. Tanya Townsend, my manager and sister in Christ, if it had not been for you I would have never been introduced to (Speakers, Publishers and Authors Association (SPAA). God has key people that he puts in your life to connect you to your next level and you were that individual. I prophesy that your book will break strongholds off of people. You just keep building that shed. LOL!!

I also want to thank you Eddie White, the next big fashion designer, for your giftedness in creating my book cover. People come in your life for a reason and I know that your passion for design is going to take you far; DON'T FORGET ABOUT ME EDO. To Joya McMillian, I so appreciate you for editing my book. You just don't know how much that blesses me; I can't wait to read your upcoming book. Dr. Michael Wilkins, founder of SPAA, thank you for listening to God to start SPAA and making opportunities available for people like me who thought I couldn't write a book. Your words of wisdom have motivated me beyond what you can imagine. BROTHER, THANK YOU SO MUCH!

Thank you Erika Gilchrist for making it possible for me to sit in your workshop on self-publishing, your information was tremendously valuable to me. To Pastor John C. Evans Jr., Rev. Yolanda Lowe (a.k.a. Mi. Low) and Apostle Matthew Stevenson, my first spiritual parents that helped groomed me into the person I am today for God. Words cannot even express how I feel about you all! Thanks to Love's Clone Publishing which and my spiritual covering Apostles Kevin & Candace Ford for your constant impartation to minister to my wife and I. We love you dearly. Finally, there will be no Joshua Cable without my proud parents Jeffrey and Velma Cable. I love you both dearly for encouraging me and supporting and raising me to be the young man I am today. I am grateful for parents that never gave up on me. Thank you.

TABLE OF CONTENTS

Introduction..10

PART ONE
The Awakening of the Kingdom Warrior

Chapter 1-The Roar of the Lord...............................14

Chapter 2-The Mind of Christ..................................22

Chapter 3-We Must Come Alive..............................41

PART TWO
The Characteristics of the Kingdom Warrior

Chapter 4-God Born Leaders...................................59

PART THREE
The Training of the Kingdom Warrior

Chapter 5-Joshua: The Great Successor..................79

Chapter 6-King David: The Young Warrior............87

Chapter 7-Gearing Up for Battle..............................92

PART FOUR
The Mandate of the Kingdom Warrior

Chapter 8-Consider Your Ways............................102

Chapter 9-Apostolic/Prophetic Decrees and Declarations..114

INTRODUCTION

"Fighters are made, but warriors are born"- Apostle Dr. Matthew Stevenson

One Saturday morning in the summer of 2010, in Chicago, I recall sitting at my desk at work. I was the only one there trying to make up some time. As I was working, the Spirit of the Lord began speaking to me about the Body of Christ. He began to reveal to me that many have become dry with their walk with God. The scripture declares that the prophet Ezekiel had a vision of a valley full of dry bones. These bones represented the children of Israel. As I sat there, he revealed to me that these bones represented many in the Church today. At one point in time the bones were a powerful army of warriors until sin entered the camp and caused these warriors to perish.

In this season of the Church, I believe the Lord is releasing a fresh anointing on the Church to be the Warrior she was meant to be. The scriptures are clear in revealing that God is a Warrior and He is leading an army. When we are born again, we join Him in this spiritual war against the Kingdom of Darkness. There are believers who started off well with God, but ended up in the valley as dry bones. The question that I ask is, "How did the Church get in the valley?" Ezekiel 37 says that the bones did not come ALIVE until the wind (Spirit) filled them. Many in the Body of Christ have a dead spirit due to the lack of submission to the Holy Spirit. This is the season where God is calling us to obey the voice of His Spirit. He wants to flow freely in our lives as it pertains to family, business, health, career, etc. We cannot be effective in the Kingdom of God without being full of the Spirit of God.

I can just imagine the soldiers in the valley fighting against their enemy, but they had no power. Do you know of people who try to do ministry without God? These individuals are simply going through the motions of Church. A spirit of Religion has bound many in generations past and present. They began to follow after false teachings and lost real joy. They were caught up more in their fleshy desires and lost focus of their real assignment as the Church; which led to being stagnated behind four walls while entertaining themselves with shouting, dancing and falling out.

This book speaks to the Body of Christ in her stage of dormancy. It is time for the Warrior to arise and to take her proper place in God's Kingdom. God is raising up "Ezekiels" in our generation to prophesy to dry bones to stir up anointings, callings, giftings and mantles for the advancement of His Kingdom. Paul, the apostle, said that he fought the good fight of faith (2 Timothy 4:7). He took his scars for Christ. I hear God saying, "WAKE UP CHURCH!" Just as John the Apostle spoke to the seven churches, the Lord is releasing prophecy to the city (local) churches of the universal Church. The body of Christ must be awakened and stirred to do Kingdom work within society. I have seen people that have a true heart to serve God, yet need anointed leaders to stand up and push them toward their destiny. Will you be the one that God will use to resurrect your brothers and sisters from the grave?

Part I

The Awakening of the Kingdom Warrior

Chapter 1

The Roar of the Lord

We are living in a very prophetic time in the history of the Church. When you look around at the universal Church, it is quite obvious that we are not operating at our greatest potential. Throughout history we have become comfortable in our 'church routine'. We arise on Sunday mornings to travel to our beautiful buildings, be entertained by the music ministry, get a thirty minute sermon that sometimes people can't relate to and we go home ready to repeat the cycle for next Sunday. We still call ourselves Christians thinking we have done what Christ has called us to do. I don't know about you, but I am tired of this flimsy Christianity. God is ready to give us the understanding of what He meant by "thy Kingdom come..." (Matthew 6:10)

A couple of years ago a movie was produced based upon the classic book "The Chronicles of Narnia: The

Lion, the Witch, and the Wardrobe written by C.S. Lewis. It is a great illustration of what is currently happening in the Spirit. It is a story about four young brothers and sisters who discover a magical wardrobe. The wardrobe takes them to a land called Narnia full of mythical creatures or ordinary animals, which are personified like humans who are under the wicked rule of the Queen of Narnia. This world awaits the fulfillment of a prophecy of two sons of Adam and two daughters of Eve to conquer the Queen of Narnia. The part of the story that sticks out to me is Aslan, a lion who represents the coming of Jesus Christ. It is an excellent allegory of spiritual warfare and the coming of Jesus to conquer evil.

In this season God is equipping the saints for the Roar of the Lord. The bible says in 1 Peter 5:8,

"Be sober, be vigilant; because your adversary the devil, as a roaring lion walketh about, seeking whom he may devour."

This verse admonishes us to be self-controlled, clear minded, and to be watchful because Satan prowls around like a lion. Pay careful attention the verse did not say that he (Satan) is a lion, but "as a lion." Our adversary has tricked many into thinking that he is a formidable lion, the king of the jungle, which is not true. The work of Satan, to kill steal and destroy (John10: 10), has been magnified because saints believe him to be a lion, but he is not, the scripture says in Revelation 5:5,

> *"And one of the elders saith unto me, Weep not: behold, the Lion of the tribe of Judah, the Root of David, hath prevailed to open the book and to loose the seven seals thereof."*

Jesus Christ is the lion. He has a real roar. As a believer, then Christ dwells within your heart. There is a roar that lives within you. This roar (sound of heaven) causes things to shake here in the earth realm. The roar is the voice of God being released to bring deliverance to the world. Unfortunately, I am led to believe that out of ignorance, we have allowed the enemy to take captive the roar of the Lord within us. If a man comes in contact with a wild animal such as a lion our natural instincts would be to fear, to run for safety. Eventually, the lion would be captured and put in a zoo or put back in the wild. If the animal were in the zoo, the animal would be tamed. Just as the lion is caged in a zoo, the enemy has convinced many in the Body of Christ to stay trapped in the spirit of religion. We have become consumed by the tediousness of church work, conferences, choir concerts and dry revival services. People are coming to the house of God gazing at the church (just like gazing at animals in a zoo) to be spectators, to be entertained. Those that are considered new members get close enough sometimes to touch and pet and eventually they too get locked up in the cage of religion. Unfortunately, there is still no release of the Roar of the Lord.

Proverbs 28:1 says,

> "The wicked flee when no man pursueth; but the righteous are bold as a lion."

Why? 1 John 4:4 says,

> "Ye are of God, little children and have overcome them: because greater is He that is in you, than he that is in the world."

It's in our nature to be bold as a lion because of the power of Christ.

The Habitat of a Lion

Let's take a moment to discuss the habitat of a lion a bit further. Why do lions roar? What is the significance? Growing up, we are all familiar with the term "King of the Jungle". The African lion is called king for a very good reason due to the fact of protecting its pride. A king protects and serves the people of his kingdom. When a lion roars it is a form of communication between them. The Lord would have us know that because He is the Lion of Judah he desires to communicate his will with the 21st Century church. Amazingly, God is in the process of raising up an army of young people to oppose the plans and purposes of the enemy. More and more I am picking up in the realm of the Spirit the hunger for God. The true worshippers are arising. Psalm 104:21 says,

"The young lions roar after their prey, and seek their meat from God."

This generation is tired of church as usual and is ready to experience the fullness of the Kingdom of God. They are ready to know their place in God's kingdom and not just on a church program; it is time to spend time preparing and doing what God has anointed us to do. The desire for the milk of the word has run dry; there is a strong desire for the meat of the word of God; food that will sustain them for the next dimension. The roar (the sound) that is being released from Heaven will communicate to this generation the very heart and mind of God.

Another interesting fact about a lion's roar is that the male has a roar that can travel up to five miles to a human ear. Lions can hear much better than humans, they are able to hear beyond the distance of five miles. By way of revelation if a lion's roar can be heard miles away before they are seen in the natural, then spiritually our enemy should fill with fear at your presence before you have fully walked into your calling. The scripture says that once Jesus Christ was born, King Herod heard that there was another King that was about to take the throne. Herod, being full of pride, jealousy and fear of losing his position, he sent out a decree to kill all male children two years old and under. That's right, King Herod had never seen Jesus, but he heard about his anointing; he heard the roar!

Satan knows that there is a roar on the inside of our spirit and it is Jesus Christ. You may not have fully begun to operate in your calling let alone even know what it is. He has a glimpse of what our destiny is and he is afraid of the advancement of the Kingdom of God through you. The kingdom has released a sound of war. Many are under attack by a Herod spirit. This principality is literally destroying many of our young people because this murderous spirit knows the calling of this generation. It is time to release the ROAR of the Lord. There is no need to fear God has a way of hiding us, while putting Satan on the run.

A lion's roar also serves as a security system for their pride when unwanted strangers infringe on their territory. This could result in some very hostile consequences if a stranger is discovered. In this last hour, it is extremely important that we feed on the Word and speak the Word. The presence of God on our lives is a must. When Jesus Christ walked the earth he spoke one word and demons were cast out. His very presence alone invoked fear in demons (Mark 5:1-13). As the Church, we must embrace the presence of God on our lives by having purified hearts. When the demons of this generation come into our presence, which should be the presence of God, it should rebuke them. Once the Word is released out of our mouth like a roar, demons are cast out. Demons have been given the right to take over our communities, homes, churches, youth, marriages finances, government, educational systems, etc. This is a result of the ignorance of man not knowing their true identity in Christ. It is time for the Roar to be released through the people of God. Not only by what we say, but also by what we do. The Bible says,

"Be doers of the word and not hearers only deceiving your own selves" (James 1:22)

Lions roar most at night when they are at their highest activity levels. When we operate in the will of God we should be running to the dark places because we want others to be set free. We are capable of sight because we have the true Light (John 1:7-9). The Bible says Psalm 119:105,

"Thy word is a lamp unto my feet and a light unto my path"

Dark places are sometimes uncomfortable; wild things come out at night. We must go in and set them free. Those in the dark are like those who are in Ps. 30 where it says,

"Weeping may endure for a night, but joy comes in the morning."

We are to introduce joy and peace to people who reside in the Kingdom of Darkness.

Small Group Discussion Questions

1. In what way have you seen yourself trapped in religion?

2. What has really hindered you from operating in your fullest potential?

3. Is there a 'roar' resounding in your spirit that will bring the Kingdom of God to where you are?

Chapter 2

The Mind of Christ

I made mention in Chapter One that the Book of Revelation says Jesus is the Lion of the Tribe of Judah. What does this mean exactly? Each of the twelve tribes of Israel had an ensign that represented them. Specifically, in the nation of Judah, the lion was the ensign on the banner. Jesus Christ came through the lineage of King David who was the king of Judah. This explains why Jesus is said to be the Lion of the tribe of Judah, the symbol for strength and a king. Jesus, as a lion, is the symbol of the king in the Kingdom of God. The king has the authority to make decrees that will establish the laws for that kingdom. This reveals the mind of the king-his thoughts, ideas, concepts, methodologies, technologies, philosophies, insights, precepts, ideologies and strategies. In the same sense, we are to submit to the mind of Christ and the mind of the Spirit in the kingdom of God. The human brain is defined as *an organ of thought and feeling: the controlling center of the nervous system in vertebrates connected to the spinal cord and enclosed in the cranium.* The mind is *the seat of thought and memory: the center of consciousness that generates thoughts, feelings, ideas, and perceptions and stores knowledge and memories.* According to Philippians 2:5, the mind of Christ is the attitude and lifestyle of Christ. In His mind you will discover His thoughts, feelings, ideas, perceptions, knowledge and memories. Malcolm X quoted, *"A mind is a terrible thing to waste"*; I wouldn't want to waste the access I have to know what Christ has for me. We experience real transformation by the renewing of our minds (Rom. 12:2). In order for us to experience the mind of Christ it must be revealed to us by the Spirit of God (1 Cor. 2:10, 11; John 16:13).

When one possesses the mind of Christ there are certain actions that will be avoided because we obtain the divine knowledge of what should be done. In other words, God gives you wisdom on how to handle things in life. Now that we have an understanding of what the mind of Christ is what is God saying to us prophetically and apostolically in this new season? The human brain is the most important organ in the body; it tells all the other parts what and when to do things. It is the Master Controller and it is broken down into three main parts: brain stem, cerebellum and cerebral hemisphere.

BRAIN STEM

This part of the brain controls heart rate, blood pressure, arm and leg movement, digestion, and basic reflexes.

1. Heart rate and blood pressure

The scripture says in Matthew 5:8,

> *"Blessed are the pure in heart: for they shall see God."*

Our hearts must be pure, right, free from any corrupt desires, so that the significance of the blood of Christ can flow in you. Blood represents life and in Christ he desires to give us abundant life. Many people haven't begun to experience this life in Christ because of sin in their lives. Today, Christ is saying LIVE in this season. LIVE in every area of your life: financially, spiritually, socially, in health, and even in your career. Live in the freedom of walking in your life's purpose as it pertains to the Kingdom of God. You are a citizen of the Kingdom of Light and therefore darkness is not your portion. When you know your identity in Him you can experience true abundant life. The Scripture says in Acts 17:28,

> *"In him we live, move and have our being..."*

2. Arm and leg movement

The Gospel of John Chapter 5 tells of a Jewish festival in Jerusalem; the particular setting takes place by a pool called Bethesda. Around the gate lay many that were sick, lame, paralyzed and blind who were waiting for an angel to come and stir the water. If anyone stepped in the pool while it was stirring would be healed of whatever disease he had. There was one man who was lame for 38 years and each time he would come to the pool someone would jump in ahead of him and he would miss his opportunity for healing. One day as Jesus was passing by, He miraculously healed the man.

We are in a season where God is saying to his people not to wait on a man to validate you. This does not mean that you are to rebel against wise council, but when God truly speaks to you and gives you an assignment you must walk in obedience. Sometimes man can talk you out of what God has called you to do. When you are on a divine assignment it doesn't make sense to the natural mind and people will fight against it. The word of the Lord has been released in the Spirit for you to use your arms and legs and take up your bed (the place where you've been asleep) and walk toward destiny. We don't have to wait another 38 years; move now and do the work of the Kingdom; pursue your purpose. He speaks to our arms and legs to move. No more impotence, blindness, lameness or excuses. Receive the healing in your spiritual arms and legs because Jesus has stirred up the water.

3. Digestion

Digestion is the process of breaking down food in order to get the nutrients from it. When we hear God's word it is like eating food. Deuteronomy 8:4 says,

> *"...man doth not live by bread only, but by every word that proceedeth out of the mouth of the Lord doth man live."*

It is very important that once we hear the Word that it begins to digest in our spirit so that we may receive all the benefits that it offers us. Luke 8:13 (LB) says,

> *"The stony ground represents those who enjoy listening to sermons, but somehow the message never really gets through to them and doesn't take root and grow. They know the message is true, and sort of believe for awhile; but when the hot winds of persecution blow, they lose interest."*

When the Word of God is not active in your life (by that I mean putting your faith to work by walking in obedience) it just sits in your spirit. Hebrews 4:2 says,

"For unto us was the gospel preached, as well as unto them: but the word preached did not profit them, not being mixed with faith in them that heard it."

The word is activated in our lives by faith; it must be rooted (digested) in order for it to prosper in your life. A good practice of getting the word rooted in you is by meditating on it. God told Joshua to meditate on His word day and night so that he would have good success in his endeavors (Joshua 1:8). In this season we want to have a smooth digestion process.

4. Basic Reflexes

A reflex is an involuntary or automatic action that your body does in response to something without you even having to think about it. We are born with most of them; they can even protect your body from things that can harm it. Paul explains in Ephesians 6:16 about the fiery darts that come our way from the enemy, we must defend ourselves against these darts. They are released to attack our spirit, but when you are motivated by your faith in God it is like a reflex. A reflex is automatic; you should automatically praise God in the good and bad. It is something that is innate in you to do. God wants us to operate in our faith more. Holding up your shield of faith will sustain you in any situation. When it seems like you are about to die, don't worry you aren't; your faith protects you in adversity. When situations come to challenge you don't worry first, TRUST HIM; it is a reflex.

Cerebellum

The next part of the human brain is the cerebellum. This part of the brain processes information having to do with our sense of balance and arm-leg coordination; it makes up one third of the total brain mass.

James 1:5-8 says,

> *"If any of you lack wisdom, let him ask of God, that giveth to all men liberally, and upbraided not; and it shall be given him. But let him ask in faith, nothing wavering. For he that wavereth is like a wave of the sea driven with the wind and tossed. For let not that man think that he shall receive any thing of the Lord. A double minded man is unstable in all his ways."*

We as Christians can sometimes be unbalanced as we walk with Christ. I believe the Lord wants his people to be balanced when it comes to us being whole in body, soul and spirit. We tend to spend more time only on one area in our lives when there should be a balance. If we are to be WHOLE (healthy) in the Spirit then we must address these three dimensions of who we are (1 Thess. 5:23; 3 John 2).

-The Body

As I have obtained more understanding of the Kingdom of God, I have come to understand the importance of taking care of my body. We don't stress enough in the Church about the importance of caring for our bodies. God is pleased when we take care of the temple that he gave us here on earth. I am quite sure that many of us have dreams and visions for our life, but if we are not healthy, how can we endure our assignment? Can you imagine a preacher trying to preach a sermon but runs out of breath during the delivery from lack of exercise? Or, maybe a singer who can't deliver effectively due to affected vocal chords from smoking or drugs?

I am not a professional nutritionist, but I can say that we have harmed our bodies by eating foods full of toxins that we were never to consume. God has given us a guide according to scripture about our diet. Just take a look at the diet of the children of Israel. When we look at research today on health and nutrition, many of the discoveries are not new. God gave his people a plan that we got away from that caused many of the diseases from the Kingdom of Darkness to come upon us.

If we eat according to God's design for us, we can avoid a lot of unnecessary medication. I believe that God is releasing divine tactics and ideas to his people on how to survive during this time of warfare on our body. Many of our sicknesses result from large quantities of unhealthy foods. In our generation it is more expensive to eat healthy, but inexpensive to eat foods that are harmful for us. If we are going to make a change, we must humble ourselves and allow ourselves to be reeducated. If you are like me, your diet is what it is because of your upbringing. Many people are enslaved by poverty and have not embraced the Kingdom. If the BODY of Christ is to finish her assignment we must take seriously the caring for of our bodies.

-The Soul

I believe that the teaching on the soul is the most neglected part of who we are. The soul is defined as the seat of our thoughts, feelings, will, and mind. The soul is what makes you, you. Our spirit can very well be functioning properly, while our soul is desperately lacking. I can attest to this. I began following Christ at the young age of twelve. As God was developing me for my ministry I noticed that I was doing a lot of spiritual things, but my soul wasn't being fed properly. There was still emotional damage, patterns of thought and selfish desires that I needed to be delivered from. The closer I got to God the more he began to set me free from the spirit of religion that entrapped me. My eyes were open to greater revelations from God about my purpose in life. It is very possible to be used by the Spirit of God to preach, flow in spiritual gifts, pray, feel the presence of God and the whole nine yards and still not be free in your soul. The bad part about this is that we are not experiencing the fullness of God. Today, ask God to set you free in your soul from unhealthy, ungodly habits and patterns of thought so that you can experience His abundant life.

-The Human Spirit

This is the part of our make-up that is connected to the Father; it is our God consciousness. We must guard ourselves closely in this area because this is where demonic spirits try to overrule. We protect this part of us when we pray, fast, study the Word of God, etc. to get closer to God. We must allow our human spirit to be guided by the Spirit of God. When we give in to our flesh we take on the wrong spirit from the Kingdom of Darkness.

CEREBRAL HEMISPHERES (Cerebral Cortex)

The largest parts of the human brain are the cerebral hemispheres. They are responsible for thought, speech, and memory. The left hemisphere is responsible for language and reasoning while the right hemisphere is responsible for spatial perceptions and creativity.

An additional part to this area of the brain is called the diencephalon. It sits between the brain stem and cerebral cortex. The other areas contained within the diencephalon are the thalamus and hypothalamus. These parts are responsible for thirst, hunger and handling emotional and sexual responses.

God wants to sharpen our language, creativity, and reasoning. The world is looking for ways to survive and when problems arise sometimes people don't know what to do. When you consider urban communities such as Chicago, New York City, or Los Angeles, there are so many problems that have arisen. I have worked in the city of Chicago where the crime rate is extremely high. Many of the citizens are living in hopelessness due to crime, poverty, and drugs. Residents are doing the best they can to cope with the rising statistics. There is a great need for creative ideas to solve problems.

I believe according to the scripture in Matthew 5:13-16 (KJV)

"Ye are the salt of the earth: but if the salt have lost its savor, wherewith shall it be salted? It is thenceforth good for nothing, but to be cast out, and to be trodden under foot of men. Ye are the light of the world. A city that is set on an hill cannot be hid. Neither do men light a candle, and put it under a bushel, but on a candlestick; and it giveth light unto all that are in the house. Let your light so shine before men, that they may see your good works, and glorify your Father which is in heaven."

Salt is good for the preservation of food. In this passage of scripture, Jesus makes it clear that the Church is the panacea to every community problem. We possess the power to bring solutions to society. Is it safe to say that the reason our communities are not where they should be is because the Church has not come into the full knowledge of her identity? Christ also calls us the light of the world. When people can't find their way in life we are able to bring them to the Light (Jesus Christ). In the Kingdom of heaven there is no need for the physical sun because the glory of God gives it its light (Revelation 21:23). Lord, let your will be done on earth as it is in heaven (Matthew 6:10).

When we share the gospel of the kingdom we introduce people to that light. Man should always see his way in the Lord. In the natural this can be related to what the Brain Center America says, *"You use mental imagery and navigation to process and rotate 2-D and 3-D objects in your mind, or to virtually move throughout an image from your surroundings which you've reconstructed in your mind. This function is very useful in everyday life -- for example, it allows you to give someone directions to your house by following the route in your mind's eye"*.[1]

The mind of the Spirit has spatial perception. Spatial perception is the ability to perceive or otherwise react to the size, distance, or depth aspects of the environment. There are times when we may receive a glimpse of what God has for us, but based on our spatial perception, it could sometimes seem so far away. As we depend on the leading of the Spirit he gives us encouragement along the way to let us know how close we are to destiny. The gift of discerning of spirits is a key gift during this phase of our walk, which helps us to find our way. During this time we must be careful because the spirit of deception's job is to make us think that we are closer than we really are. If we give in to that voice we will operate out of the timing of God.

As it relates to language, we are to speak the wisdom of God. Proverbs 24:14 says,

"In the same way, wisdom is sweet to your soul. If you find it, you will have a bright future, and your hopes will not be cut short."

The Spirit of God is the spirit of wisdom and if you tap in the Spirit then you have access to the wisdom of God. The scripture also says in James 1:5,

"Now if any of you lacks wisdom, he should ask God, who gives to all generously and without criticizing and it will be given to him"

The world needs to see this wisdom in action within the workplace, communities, government, education, media, arts and entertainment, etc. There are many stories in scripture such as Daniel interpreting the handwriting on the wall and the interpretation of dreams and Joseph interpreting Pharaoh's dreams. This took the divine wisdom of God. It resulted in them obtaining high positions in the land. Do you see how much influence we have when we speak the wisdom of God?

Obtaining this wisdom taps into the creative side of God because now we are reasoning like God. In

Genesis, we read about the creation of heaven and earth. God already had in mind what he wanted. That supernatural creative ability is in us and we can use it by the Spirit of God to accomplish our God-given assignment.

-Thirst/Hunger

> *"Blessed are those who hunger and thirst for righteousness, for they shall be satisfied."*
> *(Mat. 5:6; CSV)*

> *"Jesus answered and said unto her, If thou knewest the gift of God, and who it is that saith to thee, Give me to drink; thou wouldest have asked of him, and he would have given thee living water. The woman saith unto him, Sir, thou hast nothing to draw with, and the well is deep: from whence then hast thou that living water? Art thou greater than our father Jacob, which gave us the well, and drank thereof himself, and his children, and his cattle? Jesus answered and said unto her, Whosoever drinketh of this water shall thirst again: But whosoever drinketh of the water that I shall give him shall never thirst; but the water that I shall give him shall be in him a well of water springing up into everlasting life."*
> *(John 4:10-14; KJV)*

> *"Our fathers did eat manna in the desert; as it is written, He gave them bread from heaven to eat. Then Jesus said unto them, Verily, verily, I say unto you, Moses gave you not that bread from heaven; but my Father giveth you the true bread from heaven.*

For the bread of God is he which cometh down from heaven, and giveth life unto the world. Then said they unto him, Lord, evermore give us this bread. And Jesus said unto them, I am the bread of life: he that cometh to me shall never hunger; and he that believeth on me shall never thirst...Verily, verily, I say unto you, He that believeth on me hath everlasting life. I am that bread of life. Your fathers did eat manna in the wilderness, and are dead. This is the bread which cometh down from heaven, that a man may eat thereof, and not die. I am the living bread which came down from heaven: if any man eat of this bread, he shall live forever: and the bread that I will give is my flesh, which I will give for the life of the world." (John 6:31-35; 47-51)

In this hour, on the mind of Christ is that we hunger and thirst after righteousness. Our flesh has craved for worldly things and it has been fulfilled. We should get to a point in our relationship with Christ that we desire what he desires. As a matter of fact, in a real love relationship our desire is to not do anything that will hurt the other person. So many believers are religious with their walk with God. They religiously go to church, religiously give tithes, religiously participate in ministries and so forth and never have a relationship with God. When we draw closer to Him, we desire what he desires. David said in Psalm 37:4,

"Delight yourself in the Lord, and he will give you the desires of your heart".

God honors our desires because they are his desires. You take on his heart when you walk in obedience. Righteousness still cries out to the Body of Christ. Let the Spirit of the Lord detoxify you of all the filth from the world so that you may be filled with more of His Spirit (Eph. 5:18).

-Emotions

"There is no fear in love, but perfect love cast out fear. For fear has to do with punishment, and whoever fears has not been perfected in love." (1 John 4:18)

The more I learn about walking with Christ the more I learn about how selfish we as Christians have become. The enemy has deceived us to believe that this walk is all about us, especially in the Western Church. It is all about what we can get from God. We sometimes treat God as a genie and we forget that we are to serve others. I believe that a big reason why many Christians have not laid down their lives fully for Christ is due to fear. When we look at the lifestyle of Jesus, we are fascinated by all the great wonders that he performed, but the persecution isn't so appealing to us. Jesus was ridiculed, physically abused, and misunderstood.

One of my biggest problems with evangelism was the fear of rejection. I am a person who tries to avoid conflict, but I have learned that being a Kingdom Ambassador is very controversial. Everyone is not going to agree with you and God has a way of developing you in the weak areas of your life. Christ wants us to be perfected in love. He said that the world would know that we are his disciples by our love. We must love God and His people so much that we are willing to be persecuted for sharing the gospel of the Kingdom. The scripture teaches us in Matthew 5:11, 12,

> *"Blessed are you when they insult you and persecute you and falsely say every kind of evil against you because of Me. Be glad and rejoice, because your reward is great in heaven. For that is how they persecuted the prophets who were before you."*

For so long we have been afraid to suffer, but now is the time to ask God for a love for his people until you view suffering as a privilege.

-**Sexual Responses**

As it pertains to the Body of Christ, Christ refers to us as His bride. Since a bride is a female she is capable of reproducing. Men are naturally givers while women are naturally receivers. Intercourse between a husband and a wife is a time of intimacy. In the same sense, when we worship God it is our intimate moment with Him. Worship is a lifestyle and it shows our honor and reverence to Him for who He is. As a matter of fact, the scripture says in John 4:23,

> *"But the hour cometh, and now is, when the true worshippers shall worship the Father in the spirit*

and in truth: for the Father seeketh such to worship him."

I believe the mind of the Spirit in this hour is saying that God is or has deposited seed in our womb and we are to birth out this assignment. This seed is his Word (Luke 8:11) that is full of his revelation, thoughts, ideas, concepts, methodologies, strategies, feelings, perceptions, knowledge and wisdom.

The scripture says in Genesis 30:1 that Rachel's womb was barren and she desperately desired a baby or she would die. I think we should bombard heaven in this hour as we worship God and ask for seed lest we die and never fulfill our purpose here on earth. Look toward heaven and say, "God, give me seed lest I die!

Small Group Discussion Questions

1. Is there a word in your spirit that has been lying dormant that you have not mixed with active faith? Explain.

2. In what area of your life do you need to tap into the mind of Christ more?

3. Would you say that you are being that salt and light that God has called you to be?

4. How have you seen the wisdom of God active in your life? Local church life?

5. What seed has God planted in your spirit for Kingdom advancement?

Chapter 3

We Must Come Alive

"The hand of the LORD was upon me, and carried me out in the spirit of the LORD, and set me down in the midst of the valley which [was] full of bones, And caused me to pass by them round about: and, behold, [there were] very many in the open valley; and, lo, [they were] very dry. And he said unto me, Son of man, can these bones live? And I answered, O Lord GOD, thou knowest... Again he said unto me, Prophesy upon these bones, and say unto them, O ye dry bones, hear the word of the LORD. Thus saith the Lord GOD unto these bones; Behold, I will cause breath to enter into you, and ye shall live: And I will lay sinews upon you, and will bring up flesh upon you, and cover you with skin, and put breath in you, and ye shall live; and ye shall know that I [am] the LORD." (Ezekiel 37:1-6)

In the previous chapter we talked about the mind of Christ and discovered the revelation of each part of the human brain as it relates to the spiritual realm. In this chapter, we are going to work our way down the rest of the body and its operating systems as it relates to the Body of Christ.

Here is a story that should be familiar. The prophet Ezekiel had a vision of a valley of dry bones. The bones represented the whole house of Israel. God showed him that if he would speak life over these bones they would live. In this season I hear the Lord saying that it is time for the Church to come alive again from a state of dryness and dormancy and be active in the Kingdom of God.

As Ezekiel prophesied to the dry bones they came together; sinews and skin were supernaturally restored to the body. Would you agree with me that this process had a lot to do with the bodily systems? In order for the Body of Christ to transition from a place of stagnancy, there must be a prophetic declaration over her internal bodily systems.

"For in Him we live and move and have our being"... Acts 17:28.

In Christ there is no death, he died ONE time and now he lives forever more. In order for us to be effective we must come alive!

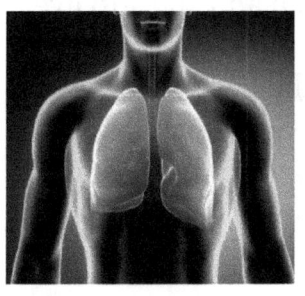

The Respiratory System The respiratory system is a system of organs in the body that are responsible for the intake of oxygen and the expiration of carbon dioxide. The prophet Ezekiel was instructed to speak to the winds of the air so that it can fill the bodies. This was a divine command for the respiratory system to come alive. In the natural we need oxygen to live; so it is in the realm of the Spirit. The scripture says in John that the Holy Spirit is like the wind. In this season we must develop a relationship with the Holy Spirit in us. The Holy Spirit is not an "IT" He is a person of the Trinity with specific roles. (John 14:26; 15:26; 16:8-14) We can see throughout the Book of Acts how the first century church heavily relied upon the Holy Spirit's guidance to advance God's Kingdom.

It is crucial that we live by the leading of the Spirit for He shall speak only what He hears the Father speak (John 16:13). In this hour of the Church, we must open our ears to hear the frequency of His voice for prophetic and apostolic direction as it relates to our lives. The Book of Revelation repeated several times the statement,

> *"He that hath an ear let him hear what the Spirit is saying to the churches"*
> *Revelation 1-3*

Living in the flow of the Spirit is like a breath of fresh air. It is refreshing to your soul and spirit to live in the fragrance of God's presence. The Spirit of Truth will help you to decipher between the false doctrines that has misled so many people. He is calling his people back to the *School of the Spirit* so that we may be reeducated with an understanding of what the Kingdom of God is all about.

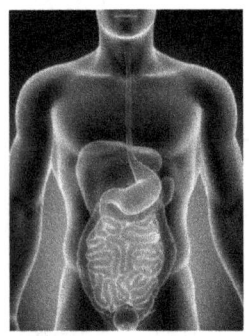

Digestive System Our human digestive system is made up of a digestive tract, which consists of the mouth, esophagus, stomach, small and large intestine, rectum and the anus. The health of our bodies is determined by good fitness and nutrition. Our bodies were made for natural foods that God planted in the earth for us to eat. It is filled with vitamins and minerals. Our spiritual body also needs vitamins and minerals and we get this from the Word of God. The scripture says in Deut. 8:1-3,

"All the commandments which I command thee this day shall ye observe to do, that ye may live, and multiply, and go in and possess the land which the LORD sware unto your fathers.

And thou shalt remember all the way which the

LORD thy God led thee these forty years in the wilderness, to humble thee, [and] to prove thee, to know what [was] in thine heart, whether thou wouldest keep his commandments, or no.

And he humbled thee, and suffered thee to hunger, and fed thee with manna, which thou knewest not, neither did thy fathers know; that he might make thee know that man doth not live by bread only, but by every [word] that proceedeth out of the mouth of the LORD doth man live."

Unfortunately, many in the Body of Christ are in a famine as it relates to revelation of the Word. So many people are hungry for more of God but leadership is not purified enough to hear from God to properly feed the sheep. I believe the Lord is releasing a Joseph anointing upon His people. This is an economic anointing where God downloads creative ideas so that we may properly prepare for the future famines. This is not just limited to food, but every sphere of society. It is a strategic move of God so that the world may see the glory of God. The saints will be prepared to flourish in the midst of a famine. Our spiritual digestive system is only activated once you eat the pure Word of God.

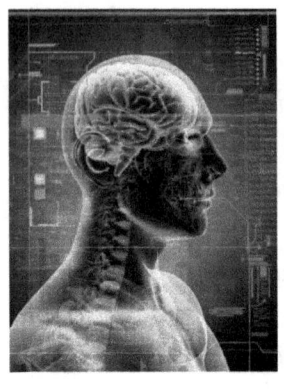

Nervous System

In chapter two we touched a lot on the brain and how it relates to the mind of the Christ. Our nervous system consists of our brain and spinal cord. We must allow Christ to activate our nervous system because after we have received the mind of Christ we must gird up the loins of our mind to prepare for the battle that is ahead of us. This mind shows that we are focused on the Kingdom of God and not the cares of this world.

The Scripture says in 1 Peter 1:13-16,

*"Therefore **gird up the loins of your mind,** be sober, and rest your hope fully upon the grace that is to be brought to you at the revelation of Jesus Christ; as obedient children, not conforming yourselves to the former lusts, as in your ignorance; but as He who called you is holy, you also be holy in all your conduct, because it is written, 'Be holy, for I am holy'.*

"This is an expression that dates back to the soldiers of the early Roman Empire. Unlike our modern soldiers, the Romans had a knee-length skirt as part of their uniforms. In the midst of battle that skirt could hinder a soldier from moving. Also, an enemy could grab the skirt as a means to gain leverage in

the attack. So the soldiers, when getting ready for intense battle, would gather and tuck the trailing skirt into their war belts. In this way they were totally free to maneuver effectively against the attack of the enemy."[2]

Guarding your mind from the attacks of the enemy will help you to maneuver against the attacks of the enemy. We are so bombarded by negative images, thoughts, and relationships that come to distract us from things of the Kingdom. Our spiritual nervous system must have an experience with the power of God to be prepared to oppose any demonic strategies.

Skeletal System

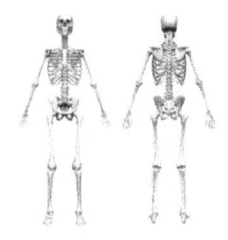

The human skeletal system serves a variety of purposes for the human body. The primary function of the human skeleton is to provide a framework for the human body. By remaining strong, the skeleton allows the body to remain upright. According to Eph. 6:13 says,

"Wherefore take unto you the whole armour of God, that ye may be able to withstand in the evil day, and having done all, to stand."

We are in a war and the only way we can accomplish our task we must stand and withstand. To withstand means to set one's self against, resist, or oppose. To stand means to continue safe and sound, stand unharmed, to stand ready or prepared. As we wrestle against our enemy, the Kingdom of Darkness, we are withstanding its schemes. After the wrestling is over, we should still be standing ready and prepared for the next battle. We are standing not in our own strength, but in the strength of Christ.

It may sound like we are to never lose a battle. Did Jesus ever lose a battle? No matter what he went through he always stood in the Spirit till the end. Even in his death, what appeared to be defeat was actually a victory. There are battles that we may seem to lose, but our battles aren't meant to defeat us but to groom us into the soldier we were born again to be.

In order for one to remain standing after a battle, our bone health must be strong. When you keep your bones strong you keep the entire body strong. Regular exercise and eating a diet high in calcium and Vitamin D will help to maintain strong bones. Scripture says in Ephesians 6:10,

> *"Finally, my brethren, be strong in the Lord, and in the power of his might".*

We must be careful not to allow laziness to overtake us. Proverbs 13:4 says,

> *"The soul of the sluggard desireth, and [hath]*

nothing: but the soul of the diligent shall be made fat."

We as believers must learn to take a punch every now and then and keep on ticking. I am led to believe that we are exalting our problems to God in prayer more than focusing on our Kingdom assignment here in the earth realm. A mature believer knows that trials come to make you strong. Have you ever had fellowship with the saints on a Sunday morning with expectations of what God was saying about your Kingdom assignment versus only coming just to be encouraged from a difficult week when will we put the devil on the run? Please don't misunderstand me, there are times when we need encouragement because of the tediousness of warfare, but don't let that be your whole walk with Christ.

I find it amazing that as we read in Ezekiel that this valley was full of dry bones. How is it that the bones of humans are the last to decompose? Why are they the strongest? According to Michelle Miley, *"Bone decomposition begins between 50 and 365 days after death, during the dry-decay stage. While acidic soils quicken the decomposition process, bones may last indefinitely in other environments if animals do not carry them away."*[3]

What does this mean by revelation? Even if you are at your lowest point and you don't feel like you are going to make it there is still some strength in you. Your job is to tap into the power source in you (Holy Spirit) and like Ezekiel watch your bones come together. We find a similar story in the scriptures of the prophet Elisha in 2 Kings 13:20, 21

"And Elisha died, and they buried him. And the bands of the Moabites invaded the land at the coming in of the year. And it came to pass, as they were burying a man, that, behold, they spied a band [of men]; and they cast the man into the sepulchre of Elisha: and when the man was let down, and touched the bones of Elisha, he revived, and stood up on his feet."

The bones of Elisha revived a dead man back to life! This man was anointed to the bone.

You are stronger than you think you are. You may be in a dry place full of bones, but those bones have endurance and once you realize that there is strength in numbers (unity) you can conquer anything. We will talk more about this in the last section.

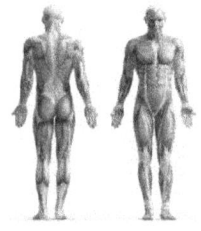

Muscular System

We have over 630 muscles in our body. Our body weight is roughly 40% muscles. Muscles allow one to move. Without them we couldn't blink, open our mouth, lift our arm or stand. There are involuntary and voluntary muscles in our body. Involuntary muscles are those muscles that are active on their own like our heart pumping or diaphragm contracting when breathing. Voluntary muscles are those muscles we have control over such as, clapping our hands, leaping, or waving our hands.

I sense in the realm of the Spirit that God wants to deal with our voluntary muscles. This is the place that cancels out stagnation. Someone that is stagnated is deficient of movement. In the Body of Christ we have been stagnated as it pertains to our Kingdom assignment. The enemy has strategically put the Body of Christ in a paralyzed state where we are not getting the full comprehension of the truth of God's word. When you are paralyzed you can only see what others are able to do. That is the person that says, "I am so proud of you. I wish I could do stuff like that", "My time of doing anything else worthwhile in life is over" or "I am just too old. " Abraham and Sarah cancelled that lie!

This lack of knowledge about the full comprehension of the truth of God's word has destroyed us because as long as we are ignorant of our Kingdom position and mandate we will continue to go in circles in the wilderness for years like the Israelites. We will continue to entertain ourselves in church services, sheep will die spiritually due to misplaced leadership, and crime, violence, poverty, and joblessness will continue to devour our communities. It's time for the Body of Christ to move forward and do what she is anointed to do. The season of stagnation is over for the Church; the season of the rise of the Kingdom warrior is here. We will affect the world to which we are called.

If we desire to see larger muscle mass we must lift weights. Larger muscle mass puts us in the position to handle more. Our spiritual muscular system must be in tact in this season because we should be able to handle more. So many times we find ourselves as believers complaining about our problems. We must mature from this place and fight like a good soldier. When you understand that you are operating in your Kingdom assignment as a warrior the Holy Spirit in you will propel you to not give up. Have you ever been in rough times and felt like giving up, but you never gave up because God had a way of encouraging you? We should rejoice because God wants us to be successful just as much as we do.

Endocrine System

The endocrine system is a very unique bodily system.

"It's a little system made up of a whole collection of glands and it does very BIG things. It regulates, coordinates and controls an extraordinary number of your body's functions. How? While your nervous system uses electricity to orchestrate all sorts of

things in your body, your endocrine system does even more through the wonder of chemicals."[4]

This system also manufactures chemicals called hormones that are released directly into our bloodstream. The term 'hormone' means to *excite* or *spur on*. They are responsible for causing other things to happen in your body. They are the key to unlocking doors to activities and making sure they are regulated. For example, controlling the regulation of body temperature or when puberty begins. I believe prophetically speaking that God is awakening this system in the body of Christ to release gifted individuals that will not only excite people but also ignite them to do the work of Christ.

There will be an anointing that rests upon them. It will begin with a small number of them, but the impact of their work will touch masses. We can see on many occasions when God used a small number of people to lead a major movement. Individuals like Noah and his family. There were only eight of them after the Great Flood and they repopulated the whole earth. Jesus and his twelve apostles being trained to establish the church as we know it or simply Jesus using a little boy's meal to feed a multitude of 5000 men.

This system is very important as well in that God will be working through people that we most likely would not expect to accomplish so much. These individuals will sometimes not be in the limelight, they may not be as educated, and they may not be old enough for it. God will orchestrate it where you will see the importance of their gifts and anointing. It could be the custodial engineer that you overlook; it could be your common teenager or the member that comes to your church regularly that sits in the back of the church. We must not overlook these individuals, as God will use them to ignite the next great move of God in your city. The scripture declares in Ecclesiastes 9:14-17,

"There was a little city, and few men within it; and there came a great king against it, and besieged it, and built great bulwarks against it: Now there was found in it a poor wise man, and he by his wisdom delivered the city; yet no man remembered that same poor man. Then said I, Wisdom is better than strength: nevertheless the poor man's wisdom is despised, and his words are not heard. The words of wise men are heard in quiet more than the cry of him that ruleth among fools."

Immune System

Your immune system is your body's natural defense against infection and illness. Specialized cells and organs all work in concert to protect your body and keep you healthy.[5] I believe this is also a very important bodily system in that it guards against false doctrines. The enemy's job is to bring all types of lies and deception to knock us off course, but in this hour God is awakening our spiritual immune system to fight off spiritual disease and sickness. It is amazing to me that out of all that Jesus Christ went through on earth he never sinned! He did not let the demonic influences cause him to fall short of the glory of God. When sin comes knocking at your door, when thoughts plague your mind we should be so in tune with the Holy Spirit that he cleans out all the filth in our hearts. Paul said it best in Romans 7:13-25 (NIV),

"Did that which is good, then, become death to me? By no means! Nevertheless, in order that sin might be recognized as sin, it used what is good to bring about my death, so that through the commandment sin might become utterly sinful. We know that the law is spiritual; but I am unspiritual, sold as a slave to sin. I do not understand what I do. For what I want to do I do not do, but what I hate I do. And if I do what I do not want to do, I agree that the law is good. As it is, it is no longer I myself who do it, but it is sin living in me. For I know that good itself does not dwell in me, that is, in my sinful nature For I have the desire to do what is good, but I cannot carry it out. For I do not do the good I want to do, but the evil I do not want to do—this I keep on doing. Now if I do what I do not want to do, it is no longer I who do it, but it is sin living in me that does it. So I find this law at work: Although I want to do good, evil is right there with me. For in my inner being I delight in God's law; but I see another law at work in me, waging war against the law of my mind and making me a prisoner of the law of sin at work within me. What a wretched man I am! Who will rescue me from this body that is subject

to death? Thanks be to God, who delivers me through Jesus Christ our Lord!

So then, I myself in my mind am a slave to God's law, but in my sinful nature a slave to the law of sin."

So you see that through Jesus Christ we can be delivered from the snare of sin; our spiritual immune system can help us fight against the flesh.

Small Group Discussion Questions

1. Are there any areas in your life where you need to make improvements as it pertains to the health of the body? If so, what are they?

2. What areas in your soul need to be healed and delivered?

3. Is there anything that you can do more to make sure your spirit is right before God?

4. How would you rate maturity in the Lord? How do you know you are mature? On a scale of 1-10 how would you rate your maturity level?

5. What causes one to lose their revival fire? How can you get it back?

6. It was stated earlier that we must be careful not to overlook the common man because they could be the one to change your city. What kinds of things keep saints stagnated in our thinking when it comes to overlooking the "common man" in our congregations?

PART II

THE CHARACTERISTICS OF THE KINGDOM WARRIOR

Chapter 4

God Born Leaders

The purpose for the roaring of the Lion is to release a war cry to a generation of dry bones. As a result of this sound, God raises up leaders to lead masses of people toward the advancement of His Kingdom. The scriptures explain this statement throughout the Book of Judges. This book of the bible is a continuation from the Book of Joshua. Joshua has died and now the Israelites are walking in disobedience to God; as a result of their disobedience, the Lord allowed their enemies to overtake them. As before the children of Israel cry out to God for deliverance. He rose up a number of judges in response.

A judge was simply a warrior ruler. God rose up these military deliverers for a particular purpose and that was to protect them against their enemies. I sense in the realm of the Spirit that the cry for these judges are being raised all around the world to deliver a people that are crying out to God for deliverance in their culture, communities, cities, nations and regions. The demonic oppression on the economy, family, government, education and other worldly systems will be highly influenced by these judges (Kingdom Warriors). The cry for deliverance has come to the ears of God. In the next couple of chapters I will make the attempt to describe the characteristics of a warrior ruler in relation to the Kingdom warrior.

Othniel (Judges 3:7-11)

Othniel, son of Kenaz, Caleb's youngest brother, was the first judge over the Israelites. A Kingdom warrior must be a person that is first chosen by the Almighty God. There is a difference between being chosen and being called by God. The scripture says in Matthew 22:14 that

> "...*many are called but few are chosen.*"

In this parable that Jesus told, only the ones that have received Christ from the call will be chosen to dwell in the kingdom. A Kingdom warrior is one that chose to wholeheartedly follow Christ.

The one God chooses is also the one that He anoints. The bible says that the Spirit of the Lord took control of Othniel. Othniel's name means *power of God*. The Spirit of God is the power of God that a believer possesses to live the life of Christ. He gives us gifts and the anointing to edify one another. He leads us into all truth and he convicts us of sin. (1 Cor. 12, John 16:8-14) You are a fool to live in this world without the Holy Ghost. You will notice on several occasions where the Church strongly depended upon the guidance of the Holy Spirit throughout the book of Acts. This Spirit took the place of Christ on earth. Whatever Christ did when he walked the earth we can do those same works and more with the Holy Spirit.

I think you may find this interesting in that Othniel reformed and purged Israel when he judged. Many of us in the body of Christ are excited about speaking in tongues, attending church conferences and revivals, choir concerts, but we are not making true disciples for the Kingdom of God. The Lord doesn't give you power for you to be slain and say that you had a good time in Church. He gives you power and authority to go and turn the world upside down (Acts 17:6). The Lord chose Othniel to serve people and bring them into destiny.

Ehud (Judges 3:15-31)

Again, we find the children of Israel enslaved by another king by the name of Eglon king of Moab. For eighteen years they are enslaved until they cry out to the Lord for deliverance. God answers by raising up Ehud. Ehud's name means *I will give thanks or I will be praised*. Another characteristic of a Kingdom warrior is that they are real worshippers and praisers. John 4:23 says,

> *"But the hour cometh, and now is, when the*

true worshippers shall worship the Father in spirit and in truth; for the Father seeketh such to worship him.

A true worshipper has a lifestyle of worship; they are not limited to being 'Sunday morning worshippers' It is a daily practice lived out through the way one treats others, through ones thought processes, entertainment and ones work ethic.

King Jehoshaphat, king of Judah (2 Chronicle 20) received news that they were about to be overtaken by outside forces. Not knowing what to do, he calls all of Judah on a fast. As a result of the fast they received a prophetic word that they didn't have to fight in the battle because it was the Lord's battle. In response to that word, Jehoshaphat organizes singers to lead the people to praise the beauty of holiness. As a result of that God caused the enemies to defeat themselves.

The Kingdom Warrior's main focus is to praise the beauty of holiness. Righteousness is his main agenda. They honor God as King of his Kingdom. In the Kingdom their needs are supplied they don't want for anything. They understand to *'seek ye first the kingdom of God and his righteousness and all these things shall be added unto you'* (Matt. 6:33). Their agenda is the advancement of the King's Kingdom. It brings great joy to their heart for others to experience the joy of the Kingdom of God.

I like the way Pastor Jack Thoemke puts it, *"Let's look at **2nd Chronicles 20:21**, it says;* **praise** *"the" beauty of holiness. In **1st Chronicles 16:29** and **Psalm 29:2**, it says;* **worship the Lord *"in" the beauty of holiness**. Praise the beauty", "worship in the beauty", see the difference here? When you worship, you are "in" the beauty, this in itself seems much deeper than praise. Let's start digging!!! The Hebrew word for praise is: hâlal, pronounced (haw-lal'). Which means; to shine; hence to make a show, to boast; and thus to be (clamorously) foolish; to rave; to celebrate, commend, glory, [sing, be worthy of] praise, rage, renowned, shine. So to praise "the" beauty of holiness is to make a show, sing, and celebrate. This is all so important but should be a stepping stone to worship. Praise with all your heart and then the next phase will be worship. Back in the day, the people would stand outside the temple praising God and waiting, as the High priest would go into the temple. The high priest was the only person that could step into the holy of holies where the altar was and into the presence of God. This would take place once a year, the priest would go in and make a sin offering for everyone and that offering would be good for one year. It would be a different high priest each year chosen by God. When God let them know who it would be, that priest would fast a couple weeks before and have everyone praying for him because if he went into the holy of holies with any sin, he would drop dead. The people would have a rope tied to his leg and he had bells on the bottom of his garment. If the people heard the bells, they knew he was dead and would drag him out. To sum it up, the people*

would "praise the beauty of holiness" and the high priest would "worship in the beauty of holiness". When Jesus died on the cross, a sin offering once and for all, the curtain that separated man from the holy of holies was torn and now, once you commit your heart to Jesus, YOU can go into the holy of holies! To sum it up: If you are born again, you can praise the beauty of holiness, then as you are focusing on God, can step into the holy of holies and worship "in" the beauty of holiness!! THANK YOU JESUS!"[6]

The scripture also states that Ehud was a left-handed Benjamite. Left-handed people are a minority in the earth today. I believe God is raising up spiritual left-handed warriors. These warriors are unique and different in the way they handle situations. Everyone may not receive them because of their standard for walking in righteousness.

The Kingdom Warrior also uses divine insight to defeat the enemy. We see that Ehud had a strategic plan in defeating the enemy. As a matter of fact he went straight for the root of the problem, which was the king himself. The Kingdom Warrior will not attempt to war without a strategic plan. In this era of hostile takeover, we as believers will no longer war without comprehension. We will be educated in strategic spiritual warfare for Kingdom results. Glory to God!

Deborah (Judges 4)

The next judge that God raises up is a woman named Deborah. Interestingly enough, she is a female, before her it was only men. I think this is significant in that God is using people we are least likely to expect. During biblical times women were on a different level as men. Women were more inferior in that culture, but Jesus broke that stereotype when he told Mary to go and share the good news about his resurrection. God is not bound by culture when it comes to whom He wants to work through. It will be men, women and children from all types of backgrounds, with all types of stories. Scripturally, we find God going beyond the kingdom of Man to work through the animal kingdom. For example, the story of Balaam and the talking donkey (Numbers 22).

In Judges 5:7, Deborah is also mentioned to be a mother in Israel,

"Villages were deserted, they were deserted in Israel, until I, Deborah, I arose, a mother in Israel"

A mother is a nurturer, one that cares for people. My wife is also a good example of a great mother to our children. She is currently a domestic custodial engineer (also known as a house wife). She labors in taking care of our children. She protects, feeds, clothes, cleans, and teaches them. The people also came to Deborah for judgment (Judges 4:5). A Kingdom warrior is a servant leader. Servant leaders are leaders who focus on the personal development of others. This leader is a servant first and then shows responsibility to people and their communities. Jesus Christ practiced servant leadership. A servant leader is not selfish; they can be compared to the function of a pastor-one whose spiritual gift is to care and nurture the flock of God through leadership. These leaders don't try to cheat you out of money just to fill their pocket. A Kingdom warrior understands ministry. God has downloaded in them the heart to lead people to the Kingdom of Light.

The story also mentions that Deborah was a prophetess. She prophesied that the victory of the children of Israel would be that of a woman by the name of Jael. Kingdom warriors are prophetic people. They carry the spirit of prophecy. The prophetic anointing brings direction, confirmation, correction, encouragement, edification and comfort.

Finally, we also see that Deborah received a word from the Lord that Barak would be responsible for gathering men for the battle with Sisera. Deborah, being a prophetess and a judge, was humbled enough not to want to get the glory. Many people want to be in the limelight. They enjoy being celebrities in the Church. I think it is key in this hour that a Kingdom Warrior maintains their humility. Again, I say take on the nature of servant. This is a person who is not jealous or envious of the other person. This person understands the power of working together as a team. A kingdom warrior knows how to submit to other's gifts and anointing to accomplish a common goal.

Gideon (Judges 6-8)

Gideon, the next judge we look at, whose name means powerful warrior or feller of trees. The story speaks of the Midianites prevailing against Israel due to the Israelite's sin against God. It got so bad that the children of Israel again cried out to God for deliverance. God in his mercy responds and gives his instructions to Gideon. We see early in the story that Gideon is threshing wheat by the winepress and God announces through an angel, *"The Lord is with thee, thou mighty man of valor."*

If you continue to read on you notice that Gideon doesn't respond like someone who would be considered a mighty man of valor; he responds as a man who is full of excuses. I think it is amazing that the people God is raising now are people like Gideon. They don't think they qualify to handle what God calls them to do. I don't think Gideon realized that he was anointed at the very moment the angel gave him the word about who he was. God had already chosen him and there was nothing he could do. I don't care how many excuses he had the angel didn't give up. God responds to the cry of his people. If you have felt a tug in your spirit to do a specific thing for God, that means that someone has been in the ear of God and he wants to use you to handle it. Kingdom Warriors are going to be people that are ordinary people who were minding their business and then God raises them up to save cities and nations.

I find it interesting that Gideon asked God for a sign (vs. Judges 6:17) not once but three times (Judges 6:36-40). You may say that Gideon didn't have faith and that he doubted himself and the Lord; well, that may be true. May I also suggest that he probably wanted to be sure that he was hearing God correctly? Let's be honest, sometimes you and I have spoken some things that we thought was the Lord and it was not. Some of us have proceeded even further and acted upon those things and was not successful. I think a Kingdom Warrior will have faith, but they will make sure they are walking in the assurance that God spoke to them. You also may say, "Well, he had an angelic visitation and God gave him the confirmation he asked for; what more does a person need? " I will argue that sometimes discouragement does try to stop you and God will give you what is needed to help you along the way. Jesus performed many miracles and there were many who still chose not to follow Him.

*"And the Lord said unto him, Surely I will be with thee, and thou shalt smite the Midianites as **one** man." (Judges 6:16)*

Now, let's think about this. Gideon was a man full of excuses and fear. He didn't think he would be able to handle the job, but God told him that he would defeat the enemy as one man. God used him to defeat this massive army (Judges 7:12) with only 300 men! Technically, can we say that the anointing on Gideon was like the strength of 300 hundred men? I believe the Kingdom Warriors that God is raising up are people with mantles that are full of power and strength. They are stronger in the realm of the Spirit than they think. We need to be careful who we put our mouth on in this hour because you may be fighting against a Kingdom Warrior who has the strength of 300 men. These men may not look physically strong and they may look nervous, but in the realm of the Spirit they will know how to wreck havoc in the Kingdom of Darkness.

Once this warrior is placed in a situation that opposes the Kingdom of God his mantle is activated and divine strength overtakes him. The scripture says in Zechariah 4:6,

> *"...Not by might, nor by power, but by my spirit, saith the Lord of hosts."*

That means that it is not human strength that we depend on but the power of God. *The Lord of hosts* is from the Hebrew name Jehovah Sabaoth which means Jehovah of the Heavenly Armies. All of heaven is backing you up when you are accomplishing a Kingdom assignment! No more punk Christians in this season; they will be sent home to watch on the sidelines, but those of the 300 will cause transformation to take place.

Another important characteristic that I see in Judges 6:34 is that Gideon blew the ram's horn when the Spirit of the Lord came upon him. As a result of this blowing of the shofar men began to be gathered to him. Kingdom Warriors will carry a heavenly sound that will gather people to follow Jesus in His army. This sound is anointed because the warrior is pure in heart before God. The people will follow the Kingdom assignment and not YOU! The heavenly sound, the anointing, the word of God that comes out of your mouth attracts people to God. The problem that we have now is people are following the man and not God. They should want to follow you because they understand that you can lead them closer to the Father.

Samson (Judges 13-16)

We now approach another popular judge over the children of Israel. Samson was a very unique individual chosen by God. The story says that his mother was barren until an angel came to her and announces that she would have a child. The instructions were,

> *"Now therefore beware, I pray thee, and drink not wine nor strong drink, and eat not any unclean thing: For, lo, thou shalt conceive and bear a son; and no razor shall come on his head: for the child shall be a Nazarite unto God from the womb: and he shall begin to deliver Israel out of the hand of the Philistines." (Judges 13:4, 5)*

God chose Samson to be a Nazarite. A Nazarite according to Numbers 6:1-21 was a person completely separated unto God. The term "nazarite" comes from the Hebrew word *nazir* meaning 'consecrated' or separated'. These individuals were made holy unto the Lord by not drinking wine, wine vinegar, grapes, raisins or intoxicating liquor. (Numbers 6:3, 4) They also could not shave their heads (Numbers 6:5) nor touch dead bodies (Numbers 6:6-7). There are a couple of revelations that I can see from this passage of scripture as it relates to the Kingdom Warrior. Samson was called and anointed from the womb. Many of the warriors that God is raising up are anointed from the womb. Their lifestyles are fully consecrated to God. These individuals are the people who get persecuted by others who say, "You think you're better than us", "It doesn't take all of that to live for God", "You are a Holy Roller", or "You are so high and mighty". You must understand that there are some people who really have a true heart for God and it won't be hard to pick them out of the crowd.

Satan understands this very well. That is why he tries to abort many babies from the womb. The angel told Samson's mother that his holiness would not just be that he was a believer of God but the abstaining of alcohol, the cutting of his hair and not touching the dead demonstrated it. Do you know the effects of alcohol on an unborn fetus?

"A woman who drinks alcohol while she is pregnant may harm her unborn baby (fetus). Alcohol can pass from the mother's blood into the baby's blood. It can damage and affect the growth of the baby's cells. Brain and spinal cord cells are most likely to have damage.

The term "fetal alcohol spectrum disorder" (FASD) describes the range of alcohol effects on an unborn child. The problems range from mild to severe. Alcohol can cause a child to have physical or mental problems that may last all of his or her life.

The effects of alcohol can include:

- Odd facial features. A child may have a small head, flat face, and narrow eye openings. It may be hard to pick out one trait, but in general, a child's head and face just don't look right. This gets more obvious by age 2 or 3.

- Growth problems. Children who were exposed to alcohol in the womb may be smaller than other children of the same age.

- Learning and behavior problems.

- Birth defects. Problems can occur that involve parts of the body such as the eyes, ears, heart, bones, or urinary tract.

- Heavy alcohol use during pregnancy can also lead to miscarriage, stillbirth, or a baby being born early."[7]

Could you imagine what would have happened if Samson's mother would have drank alcohol during her pregnancy. Not only would she be walking in disobedience but also the consequences of that would have distorted God's plan over Samson's life. What am I saying? The enemy knows the power of a

Kingdom Warrior so he attempts to even destroy them from the womb. Do you have any idea as to how many potential Kingdom Warriors could have been born if they were not aborted?

Let me give a personal testimony. Around the year 2009, I was still living in Mississippi, and I was sitting at the front desk at work. God began to give me further understanding behind the meaning of my name. The name Joshua means *Jehovah is salvation*; it is also the Hebrew name for Jesus. Aloysius, my middle name, means *famous warrior* and Cable means *rope maker*. As you can see, it is in my nature to be a warrior. Joshua saves, Aloysius is famous and Cable is responsible for binding demonic forces.

I was so stirred by this that I called my mom immediately to tell her what I discovered. She responded by saying when she was pregnant with me out of wedlock one of her aunts tried to encourage her to get an abortion; it was a demonic plot to hide it from my grandmother. Fortunately, my mom said no. I was around 26 or 27 years old when she revealed that to me. Did I get angry? Of course not! I actually rejoiced because what the devil tried to do it didn't work and I would not be writing this book right now if I were dead. Kingdom Warriors are a main target of the enemy and if you are a parent right now protect the anointing on your children's life. They have a mandate from God.

Another characteristic that we can find in a Kingdom Warrior is found in Judges 14& 15. We can see from these two chapters that Samson tackles a young lion and rips his jaws apart; he also defeats 1000 men with the jaw of a donkey. The scripture says that the Spirit came upon him and he was able to FEARLESSLY accomplish his assignment. God is raising up fearless Kingdom Warriors. Many of us have fear on some level. The scripture says,

> "For God has not given us a spirit of fear and timidity, but of power, love, and self-discipline"
> (2 Timothy 1:7-NLT)

Fear is from the enemy. It will stagnate one from progressing in life. I believe that this is one of the main demonic strongholds that a Kingdom Warrior will be attacked by in some way. Here is why:

"The spirit of fear is released to attack the peace, courage, vision, and faith of individuals, creating a debilitating stronghold in their mind. It also has the power to abort purpose, derail divine destinies, and assassinate future hope and faith in the power of God. It is of extreme importance to comprehend the insidious nature of this spirit relative to our future, because the way we perceive or think about the future actually sculpts and contours how we handle the present. Fear comes from the root word phobos, which means, "that which may cause flight". This is also where we get the word phobia, which is a persistent irrational fear of something that is so strong that it compels us to avoid the object of the fear. It is a psychological reaction to something or someone who poses a threat to our sense of security

and safety. It also denotes emotional unrest and "dis-ease" caused by uncertainty of one's ability to overcome situations and challenges in life-financial, spiritual, physical, social, material, psychological, or emotional disability...There are different degrees of fear:

Alarm: initial realization of danger

Fright: sudden and momentary

Dread: stronger in intensity, dread grips the heart as it anticipates impending events that are difficult or impossible to avoid, rendering the person helpless and powerless over it.

Terror: overpowering, intense, and debilitating

Horror: a combination of fear and aversion

Panic: sudden, frantic fear that robs a person of reason

Dismay: apprehension that robs a person of courage and power to act efficiently and effectively

Consternation: a state of often paralyzing dismay characterized by confusion and helplessness

Trepidation: dread characterized by trembling[8]

If we are going to defeat the demonic forces of this generation we must take courage and go forth with the knowledge of who we are. Samson knew that he couldn't be defeated because he was in the will God.

It was not natural strength, but supernatural strength. With God all things are possible (Matt.19: 26)

In Judges 16, we find Samson walking in disobedience to God. As a result he lost the source of his power, his vision and now he is in a stronghold. Being separated from the presence of the Lord due to sin will put you in a state of vulnerability. Many of those in leadership are just like Samson in that the spirit of lust has overtaken them and left them in torment. The spirit of adultery, homosexuality and fornication has destroyed many churches and families in our generation. In spite of his downfall, Samson's hair began to grow back. He saw an opportunity to finish what he started. In a Kingdom Warrior there is still the ability to come back alive in the realm of the Spirit. If you are willing to do what 2 Chronicles 7:14 says,

"If my people, which are called by my name, shall humble themselves, and pray, and seek my face, and turn from their wicked ways; then will I hear from heaven, and will forgive their sin, and will heal their land"

Then you can finish what you started and put an end to the laughter of the enemy over your life.

Small Group Discussion Questions

1. In what way have you mishandled the power of God (Othniel) in your life?

2. What are your thoughts on 'praising the beauty of holiness' and 'worshipping in the beauty of holiness'?

3. How strategic have you been in your sphere of influence when it comes to advancing the Kingdom?

4. Where in your life have you made excuses for not accomplishing the will of God for your life?

5. In what ways have you served as a servant leader? Where have you fallen short of not operating as a servant leader?

6. Have you ever been discriminated against that may have caused you to not fulfill a particular assignment?

7. Discuss areas in your life where you need a greater consecration.

8. Share your testimony in where you felt the enemy laugh over your life.

Part III

The Training of the Kingdom Warrior

Chapter 5

Joshua

The Great Successor

It is very important that you understand that when God calls you to something there is a process of development. I think many believers in this era don't like process. Many of the sermons and gospel music promote the message that God is going to bring you out of the adversity that we encounter. Although this is very true, however, it will be done on His time and not ours. The reason is to prepare you for the prophecy that He has spoken over your life. If we are honest with ourselves much of what God promised us that we will have or do we may not be able to handle it at that time.

Therefore, God takes us through a stage of

development to make sure our motives are right toward Him so that he will get the glory in the end. Our mind is too finite to fully understand God; that is why we need the mind of Christ to understand what God is doing with us. If we understand that He is developing us for the better we should be able to endure adversity a little while longer and like the discipline and pruning that he takes us through. Is the process easy? No, it is not but it is worth it. The saying is, "No pain, no gain".

Furthermore, a Kingdom Warrior, as important as his assignment is, must undergo a training process. Proverbs 24:6 (NIV) says,

"for waging war you need guidance and for victory many advisors".

If we are going to succeed in this warfare we must submit to wise godly counsel. Everyone has a different development season. We aren't all necessarily called to the same thing, so God trains us in different ways. He trains you for what you are called to do. The way God trains and develops us is through fiery situations; things that make us feel uncomfortable. These trials build character in us. I think we should find that encouraging because if you feel like you are about to die in the fire you aren't because God trusted you with the trial.

I want to look at two types of individuals in scripture who are good examples of being developed as a Kingdom Warrior. The first person is Joshua, the son of Nun, a very well known individual in scripture. We all know him as the one whom God used to lead the Israelites to shatter the walls of Jericho, to defeat the king of Ai and lead the Israelites to the Promised Land. Before Joshua accomplished all his conquests God took him through a development stage. We first see Joshua in Exodus 24:13 on the mountain with Moses as his minister. To be a minister simply means one who serves. The training of a Kingdom Warrior is one who has a heart to serve others. The real servant is the one who doesn't long to be in the limelight, but wants to be sure that the Kingdom of God is advanced. Let God be responsible for making you famous and you focus on making God famous to those who don't know Him. He told Abraham,

"I will make you into a great nation, I will bless you, I will make your name great and you will be a blessing." (Genesis 12:2)

Not only was Joshua a minister to Moses, but we can also see that Joshua was submitted to him. (Exodus 17:9) A big issue with many people in the body of Christ is the lack of submission to those in leadership. First and foremost, we must be submitted to God our Father. James 4:7 says,

"Submit yourselves therefore to God. Resist the devil and he will flee from you."

Submit means to yield to one's admonition or advice; obey. Just as we are to submit to the Father, we must also submit to those that He has placed in our lives for Kingdom growth. Our problem is that we don't like people telling us what to do. When you submit to your spiritual leaders they will sometimes tell you to do things that you don't want to do. You may not like it, but it is okay because it is meant to better you as a disciple. Kingdom Warriors must pass the submission test before they can be successful. Exodus 17:9, 13-14 also shows Joshua taking orders from Moses to battle Amalek. As he walks in obedience he is successful in this endeavor.

I am reminded of an instance when my pastor in Jackson, Mississippi, was training me on being a more effective preacher. He taught me about the importance of being sensitive to the Holy Spirit and to people when it came to delivering the message of the Lord. One of the important dynamics of speaking is recognizing when you have spoken too long; therefore losing your audience's attention. I was asked to conduct a funeral for one of our teenagers at our church. The young boy died in a major car accident and the mother requested that I do the eulogy.

The young teenage boy was highly influential. This was obvious from the many students and teachers who came out to support. The sanctuary was packed to capacity with many ethnicities. We had a large sanctuary so it held plenty of people. Well, I didn't know too much about this young man to speak personally about his life, so I spoke to the audience what God gave me. The power of God moved so in that place that over 100 young people were converted!

I only spoke for about 15 minutes. Submitting to my pastor's leadership and guidance on ministering to such a crowd opened doors for many students to get delivered. Submitting to authority is crucial for your development as a Kingdom Warrior.

We also notice that Joshua went to the mountain with Moses in the presence of God. We can also see in Exodus 33:11 that Moses left the presence of God, but Joshua stayed behind to dwell a little while longer. I think this is key for a Kingdom Warrior in that he lives in the presence of God; they are throne dwellers. A Kingdom Warrior has longevity in prayer. They don't rush their private prayer time in order to get to the next thing on their list. This time is precious to them and to God because they understand that the place of prayer is what causes them to thrive in the realm of the Spirit.

As God rises up this warrior he will have a hunger for the presence of God. When others are longing to be with other people and do other activities you will notice a Kingdom Warrior will stress the importance of his prayer time. Please don't misunderstand me; it is important to function outside of the spiritual realm, but the heart of a Kingdom Warrior can't properly rest until they spend that time with the Father in order to gain insight about their journey.

In Exodus 32:17-18, Moses and Joshua are making their way down the mountain from receiving the Decalogue. Before they arrive to where the

Israelites were, Joshua makes a statement in verse 17,

"...There is a noise of war in the camp".

I find this interesting because if you continue to read the story there was no war, but the shouting of the people reminded Joshua, a warrior, of the sound of war. Kingdom Warriors are always on post for any type of spiritual warfare that could break out. It is imbedded in their nature to stand guard; a Kingdom Warrior will be ready to intercede when necessary. God has to train these individuals to tune their spiritual ear to hear.

"He that hath an ear, let him hear what the Spirit is saying to the churches" (Rev. 3:22)

These are the individuals you can count on to pray when things get a little rough in your life.

Finally, In Numbers 14:1-9, we see the Israelites grumbling against Moses about their exodus from Egypt. In their mind they didn't think God was really on their side to protect them from their enemies. When Moses and Aaron heard their complaints, they fell on their faces, but it was Joshua and Caleb who rent their clothes. Joshua and Caleb were two of the twelve spies who sought out the Promised Land. The congregation didn't think they could defeat their enemies in Canaan. It brought sorrow to Joshua and Caleb's heart to hear the doubt from the Israelites. Joshua and Caleb began to motivate the people, but the people didn't want to hear it.

I think apart of the training of a Kingdom Warrior is to see if they are able to stand in spite of opposition. When no one else is willing to believe what God said, are you still willing to fight in order to possess what God says is yours? When people tore their clothes in the bible it was an outward sign of mourning over someone's death, righteous anger or deep grief over a disaster. I believe Joshua had a righteous anger. It should be embedded in the spirit of a warrior to hate sin and be willing to fight the good fight faith.

Small Group Discussion Questions

1. Are you in a development season? How do you know? What are your experiences like?

2. Have you ever been tempted to rush the development season to get to the promise? Share an experience of when you rushed the development season and tried to do things in your own power.

3. Describe your personal devotional life

Chapter 6

King David - The Young Warrior

We now come to another famous warrior in the bible by the name of David. As opposed to Joshua we are given more detail about his upbringing and development as a warrior. In 1 Sam. 16:18, 21; 17:15, we find David having to manage a number of roles. He was a shepherd, a musician, armor bearer, a man of war; he also was wise, handsome, strong and most of all anointed. I find this interesting in that developing into God's warrior; you must be able to handle a number of tasks.

Before I moved to Chicago, I was a very busy young man. I was a part time seminary student, a youth pastor, a District Director of Evangelism, an itinerant preacher, a husband, and had an 8 to 5 job. Yes, my plate was full. There were times when I felt like giving it all up. On top of that, I was talented in singing, dancing and playing the viola! When you are gifted like that people pull you left and right. There were two things I had to learn from this: 1) God taught me what I am not 2) being involved in so many things that is not connected to my destiny was a distraction. However, I do believe that God will entrust you with many jobs to train you for where you are going. Due to my experience in these areas I am qualified to help others build their ministries. A Kingdom Warrior must be versatile at times so they can combat a variety of areas in the Kingdom of Darkness.

Another part of a Kingdom Warrior's training is the development of confidence. If you are going to be on God's team there will be many obstacles that come your way to challenge your confidence. David had the opportunity to defeat Goliath and he did it with much confidence. I believe David was confident because God was training him on the backside of the desert to kill bears and lions. God understood the ranking that David would have in the realm of the Spirit and in order for him to conquer a giant like Goliath his training had to be intense.

Each situation David encountered made him stronger in his confidence; so by the time he encountered Goliath it was not a hard challenge to defeat him. A Kingdom Warrior must undergo tests that will build up confidence. Many of us are fearful to tackle certain issues and Godly assignments because we are not confident. Once you overcome any trial it equips you for another trial that is similar to it. Goliath appears to be strong just like the bear and lion, but the only difference was that he was taller. Many times our problems get bigger, but if you allow God to process you, you will be fit to handle anything he allows to come your way. (1 Sam. 17:37)

During your training as a Kingdom Warrior, God will cause you to have relationships with people that will develop, guide, and protect you along the journey. David and Jonathon had such a relationship (1 Sam. 18:1-4). A true love relationship with another brother or sister is important to help you to be accountable. We must guard ourselves against isolation. Isolation is a trick of the enemy to keep you away from those that can help mold you into who you are supposed to be. During this season of my life I have been challenged to develop deeper relationships with people for my development. I had a struggle developing close relationships with men in particular due to my past experiences. God has been faithful in helping me to overcome this obstacle. The more I embrace it the more healing I experience within my soul. You can't live this Christian life stuck in your house and never come out to fellowship. Many of your needs are supplied from simply developing relationships.

And finally, if you are a warrior with any type of purpose you must undergo the test of being attacked by a Saul spirit. It is this spirit that recognizes the anointing on your life and out of jealousy it desires to kill you and your purpose so that it can remain in authority. The challenging part is that you must maintain your integrity and not attack because it comes through anointed leadership. David had experienced this. The Lord anointed King Saul to lead the Israelites, but because of his disobedience God rejected him. God chose David to be the next king. Saul recognized the anointing on David and saw how people gave him more credit than himself. In spite of all that Saul tried to do to kill David, David never retaliated to kill him. Can you still be submitted to leadership that doesn't respect the anointing on your life? Can you wait until God positions you to take your place in the face of your enemy?

Small Group Discussion Questions

1. Have you ever had to serve under a Saul that didn't respect the call on your life? If so, share your experience.

2. Have you battled with developing meaningful relationships? Explain.

3. Do you have experiences that have challenged confidence in yourself?

Chapter 7

Gearing Up for Battle

Once the Kingdom Warrior has been awakened and trained he must be geared for battle. Paul, the apostle, explained well what that would look like in the realm of the Spirit. In Ephesians 6:14-18, we find the description of the armor for the Kingdom Warrior.

Belt of Truth

Paul begins by talking about the belt of truth. This was usually the first piece of clothing that was put on the soldier. It was a wide and strong belt. The belt wrapped around a loose tunic that provided freedom of movement. The belt gave support to the abdominal muscles and sometimes had a scabbard for the sword. I sense in this hour that the Spirit of truth desires to expose all false doctrines or doctrines of devils that has had any impact in our lives in order to superimpose it with godly truth. Paul encouraged

Timothy to study to show himself approved (2 Tim. 2:15). The Lord is reeducating his people by way of the "School of the Spirit" to make sure we are properly ready to war. He is taking us back to foundational truth as it relates to our mission as believers. This belt of truth helps keep things from falling apart. Many churches and ministries are falling apart because of the lack of truth. It is the truth that will make you free. (John 8:32) We must use discernment in this season against the angel disguised as an angel of light.

Breastplate of Righteousness

The next piece of armor is the breastplate. There were two types of breastplates: some were made out of leather and some were made from small interwoven brass rings. The soldiers that were considered high ranking would sometimes have breastplates of a single piece of molded bronze. Bronze was a lightweight metal and its purpose was to protect the vital organs of the body.

A Kingdom Warrior that wears a breastplate of righteousness has to be righteous. The breastplate covers the chest and every organ underneath it: heart and lungs. We must guard our heart in this battle. The enemy releases demonic spirits to feed into our motives. Walking righteously keeps our hearts pure before God (Mat. 5). Our righteousness keeps us alive: we breathe with our lungs and our heart pumps blood to keep us alive. Righteousness will keep us from going to sleep in the Spirit or becoming too dry.

We must awake and arise in righteousness. I must guard my eyes, mouth, ears, and nostrils because these are entrances to my heart.

As a Kingdom Warrior, I am instructed to stand. I stand with armor in place. As long as I stand my ground in Christ every device that the enemy sends my way will not prosper. (Isaiah 54:15-17). Sometimes these weapons will appear to self-destruct when you rebuke them or sometimes it may touch you, but it won't kill you. When he, the enemy, comes in like a flood the Spirit of the Lord lifts up a standard against him. (Isaiah 59:19)

Shoes with the Gospel of Peace

The shoes of a Roman warrior were made like a sandal. The sandals had thick leather soles held together by small nails that provided protection for hand-to-hand combat. The shoe was held securely by a leather strap that was positioned above the ankle.

When we look around the world many people are living lives that are disturbing. There is sex trafficking, divorce, unjust government, or fathers not fulfilling their duties. The responsibility of a Kingdom Warrior is to carry the gospel of peace to the world. The anointing that rests on a Kingdom Warrior will break the tormenting spirits in order to release the God kind of peace. According to Isaiah 61:1 where it says,

"The Spirit of the Lord GOD [is] upon me; because the LORD hath anointed me to preach good tidings

unto the meek; he hath sent me to bind up the brokenhearted, to proclaim liberty to the captives, and the opening of the prison to [them that are] bound"

Kingdom Warriors are anointed to set people free.

Jesus said in the Gospel of John 16:33,

"These things I have spoken unto you, that in me ye might have peace. In the world ye shall have tribulation: but be of good cheer; I have overcome the world."

John 14:27,

"Peace I leave with you, my peace I give unto you: not as the world giveth, give I unto you. Let not your heart be troubled, neither let it be afraid."

The world has tribulation, but in the Kingdom of God there is peace. Everywhere the soles of a Kingdom Warrior goes brings peace. If people ever have to complain about your presence then you may not be bringing the peace of God to the atmosphere. We must put on our shoes so that we can take peace to areas that are not experiencing it.

Shield of Faith

In the Roman army, soldiers were also equipped with a small round shield and large rectangular ones. The large one in particular stood about four feet tall and two feet wide. The shield was made of layers of laminated wood covered by linen and leather. Along the edges of the shield, it was covered in brass or bronze that protected it against sword attack. It also had designs of traditional Roman symbols such as eagle's wings or lightning bolts. The primary use of the shield was for individual protection but the soldiers were also able to unite to form a large wall of protection.

It is by faith that the Kingdom Warrior is able to block the arrows of the enemy. There are many arrows of our day that are programmed to hit our spirit. Darts of negativity, ill spoken words, fear, malice, and the list goes on. Our faith in God is more powerful than we realize. In the Book of Hebrews 11, we can read about the wall of fame of people who were known for their faith in the Almighty God. They overcame obstacles because they believed and trusted God. We must be able to trust God in spite of what our culture says.

James 2:26 says,

> "For as the body without the spirit is dead, so faith without works is dead also."

God doesn't want us to declare that we have faith without works attached to it. In this warfare, we must declare the name of the Lord while charging the gates of hell. Hell will release an attack on your prophecy from God but if you stand with your shield of faith it will block your spirit from receiving any news from hell. I encourage you to make a move of faith in this season of your life toward that dream or vision. Block all lies and keep fighting until you have victory.

Helmet of Salvation

The Roman soldier's helmet was usually made of bronze and sometimes of leather or iron. The helmet protected the sides of the face with "cheek pieces" that was connected to each side secured under the chin by leather straps. The helmet was equipped with something called a 'shelf' that protected the back of the neck and shoulders to protect the soldier from arrows.

The helmet for the Kingdom Warrior symbolizes that if you are going to operate in God's army you must be saved for real. There are many people who are going through the motions of "Church" but don't have a true relationship with Christ. Many people have come to our altars confessing Jesus Christ as Lord but never left the altar to follow Him. When Jesus called his disciples they left all and followed him. There is an assurance on the part of the Kingdom Warrior to know that they are believers. They graduate from the level that says, "Am I really saved?" When the enemy sees the helmet he knows that he is battling a real believer. Whatever you do, don't let the devil knock off your helmet.

In Exodus 28:36-38 (KJV), it reads,

"And thou shalt make a plate [of] pure gold, and grave upon it, [like] the engravings of a signet, HOLINESS TO THE LORD. And thou shalt put it on

a blue lace, that it may be upon the mitre; upon the forefront of the mitre it shall be. And it shall be upon Aaron's forehead, that Aaron may bear the iniquity of the holy things, which the children of Israel shall hallow in all their holy gifts; and it shall be always upon his forehead, that they may be accepted before the LORD."

Just as the priest in the Old Testament wore a headpiece that showed that they were separated for the work of God this helmet reminds the enemy that you are righteous. Again I say, don't let the devil knock off your helmet! If you have no helmet, there is no access to power to combat the enemy effectively.

The Sword of the Spirit

The Roman soldier carried a small dagger and a large two-edged sword. The large sword was usually 24 inches long and 2 inches wide with parallel sides. This weapon was developed after the Romans learned of the effectiveness of the smaller sword. Although formerly, the swords were larger, but the newer swords were shorter and more pointed. A 'piercing' sword was more effective.

The scripture in Matthew 4, talks about how the Devil set out to tempt Jesus after his 40 day fast. Three times the Devil attempted to deter Jesus but Jesus being the Word of God spoke the Word of God to defeat the enemy. It is imperative that the Kingdom Warrior use the word of God to ultimately defeat the enemy. Once you move with your shield of faith to block the fiery darts of the enemy, you defeat the enemy by using God's word. The bible says,

"For the word of God is living and active. Sharper than any double-edged sword, it penetrates even to dividing soul and spirit, joints and marrow; it judges the thoughts and attitudes of the heart."
(Hebrews 4:12-NIV)

The word of the Lord is sharper than any man made sword. When God speaks it has creating and transformation power. It penetrates to the very core. The enemy becomes feeble when the spoken word of God is manifested.

I encourage you in this season to gird yourself in the Spirit with your armor if you want to be effective in the Kingdom. The lack of proper preparation will make you a prime target for the enemy.

Small Group Discussion Questions

1. Can you truthfully say that you are wearing every piece of the warrior's garment? Which piece are you lacking?

2. How does one really know they are a disciple of Jesus Christ?

3. Where in your life have you only spoken things by faith and not acted upon them?

PART IV

THE MANDATE OF THE KINGDOM WARRIOR

Chapter 8

Consider Your Ways

Once the warrior has been awakened, trained and geared it is now time to take real action. Unfortunately, for so long many believers have never graduated past the training and never operated in being who they really are. I want to observe a very familiar passage of scripture that relates to where I see the Church currently.

"Thus speaketh the Lord of hosts, saying, This people say, the time is not come, the time that the Lord's house should be built. Then came the word of the Lord by Haggai the prophet, saying, Is it time for you, O ye, to dwell in your ceiled houses, and this house lie waste? Now therefore thus saith the Lord of hosts; Consider your ways. Ye have sown much, and bring in little; ye eat, but ye have not enough; ye drink, but ye are not filled with drink; ye clothe you,

but there is none warm; and he that earneth wages earneth wages to put it into a bag with holes. Thus saith the Lord of hosts; Consider your ways. Go up to the mountain, and bring wood, and build the house; and I will take pleasure in it, and I will be glorified, saith the Lord. Ye looked for much, and, lo it came to little; and when ye brought it home, I did blow upon it. Why? Saith the Lord of hosts. Because of mine house that is waste, and ye run every man unto his own house. Therefore the heaven over you is stayed from dew, and the earth is stayed from her fruit. And I called for a drought upon the land, and upon the mountains, and upon the corn, and upon the new wine, and upon the oil, upon that which the ground bringeth forth, and upon men, and upon cattle, and upon all the labour of the hands." (Haggai 1:2-11 KJV)

The purpose of the Book of Haggai was to awaken God's people to rebuild the temple. From the passage, we see that the people didn't discern the timing of the Lord to rebuild it, but they had plenty of time to invest in their own agenda. Due to their lack of commitment to the work of the Lord, it brought a curse upon them and their land. Twice God responds, "Consider your ways". I hear this phrase ringing in my spirit as it rings in the heart of God. It is understood that a physical building is needed to be rebuilt here, but coming from a New Testament perspective, scripture says in 1 Corinthians 6:19,

"What? Know ye not that your body is the temple of

> *the Holy Ghost which is in you, which ye have of God, and ye are not your own?"*

> *"Ye also, as lively stones, are built up a spiritual house, an holy priesthood, to offer up spiritual sacrifices, acceptable to God by Jesus Christ." (1Peter 2:5)*

> *"Know ye not that ye are the temple of God, and that the Spirit of God dwelleth in you? If any man defile the temple of God, him shall God destroy; for the temple of God is holy, which temple ye are." (1 Cor.3: 16, 17)*

I want to propose that in this hour God isn't concerned about a 'building' per se, but he is concerned about the actual 'Church'; his temple. I want to challenge us in our thinking in this last section of the book to really rethink what we know as 'Church'. Our 'temple' has been ruined physically, emotionally, spiritually, socially, mentally, etc. We, like the people in the book of Haggai, have invested in our own agenda of Church and have neglected who we are as a whole in our communities. We are not producing real disciples; therefore we are not salt and light. I believe the Spirit of God is leading us to focus our attention on the uniting of the Body. For years, we have seen much division in the Church and if we want to see a mighty move of God it is going to come from an army working together as one. I want to experience the 'dew from heaven' as it was in scripture. Consider your ways Church!

WHAT or **WHO** is the Church?

Believe it or not, the term *church* was around before Jesus introduced it to his apostles. Below you will find a detailed description of this concept of *church:*

"The new Webster's International Dictionary, 1909 edition, gives this definition of the word: "Church (church), n. [ME. chirche, fr. AS. circe, fr. Gr. kyriakon the Lord's house, fr. kyriakos concerning a master or lord, fr. kyrios master, lord, fr. kyros power, authority; akin to Skr. gram mighty, bold Olr. caur, cur, hero. Cf. KIRK.] 1. **A building** set apart for public worship, esp... 2. **A place** of worship of **any** religion, as, **formerly**, a Jewish or **pagan temple** or a mosque. Acts 6:37."

There were pagans using the word "church" long before Christians ever began using it. The word "church," originated from the Greek word "kuriakon," which later evolved to chirche and to "church" in English. To the pagans the word kuriakon meant "belong to the lord", it was a house or building representing their pagan lords in which they met.

"CHURCH: From the Greek kuriakee, "house of the Lord," a word which passed to the Gothic tongue; the Goths being the first of the northern hordes converted to Christianity, adopted the word <u>from the Greek Christians of Constantinople</u>, and so it came to us Anglo-Saxons (Trench, Study of Words). But Lipsius, from circus, from whence kirk, a circle, because the oldest temples, **as the Druid ones**, were circular in form." (Fausset's Bible Dictionary)

The early assembly of believers did not have a clergy distinct from the rest of the body. Clergy with titles and authority was foreign to the early disciples. It was the rise of this authoritarian clergy that needed a building to control the people both religiously and politically and to gather the people around the clergy. The Catholic Church and the Church of England both used the word "church" and its meaning as a building to hold the people in subjection to their control. Without a building the clergy would have lost their power over the people. Even today, without a building the clergy system would fall. This system of clergy/laity and the use of a building is what we have come to know as the "institutional" church system. This system was **totally** foreign to the vocabulary and the life of the disciples of Jesus, who built and depended on the move of the Holy Spirit through **all** the people being built together. Therefore the retaining of the word "church" in our translations of the bible became crucial for the survival of the institutional church system even to this day."[9]

"YEAR AND VARIOUS FORMS OF THE WORD

1600 church becomes common spelling during long process of standardization.
1500 church, churche, chirch, chirche, chyrch, chyrche, cherche
1400 churche, chirch, chirche, chyrch, chyrche, cherch, cherche
1300 churche, chirch, chirche, chyrch, chyrche, cherch, cherche
1200 churche, chureche, churiche, cherche, chereche, chyrche, chyreche, chireche, chiriche, chirche
1100 chirche, chiriche, chireche, chyreche, chyrce (Middle English period 1100-1500)
1000 cirice, cyrice, circe, cyrce, kirk (Old English/Anglo-Saxon period 600-1100)
300+ kirika, kerika (W. German/Old Saxon—Pre-English period)
200+ kyriaka/kuriaka, kuriakon (Greek) And when you consider the history of the word it is just as obvious, that it is no accident this is the meaning being conveyed. It cannot be stressed to strongly that wherever we find "church" in scripture it is never *kurakon* that we find in the original Greek. The New Testament writers chose *ekklesia* because it clearly defines those called out of the world to assemble in Christ.

Strongs # 1577-- *ekklesia*
From a compound of # 1537- *ek* (out) and a derivative of # 2564- *kaleo* (to call) = *ekklesia*

A gathering of citizens called out from their homes into some public place, an assembly.

a) an assembly of the people convened at the public place for the purpose of deliberating.

b) the assembly of the Israelites

c) any gathering or throng of men assembled by chance, tumultuously

d) in a Christian sense:
1) an assembly of Christians gathered for worship in a religious meeting.
2) a company of Christian, or of those who, hoping for eternal salvation through Jesus Christ, to observe their own religious rites, to hold their own religious meetings, and to manage their own affairs, according to regulations prescribed for the body for order's sake.
3) those who anywhere, in a city, village, constitute such a company and are united into one body.
4) the whole body of Christians scattered throughout the earth.
5) the assembly of faithful Christians already dead and received.
(Thayer's Greek Lexicon

The New International Dictionary of New Testament Theology.
ekklesia, centuries before the translation of the OT and the time of the NT, was clearly characterized as a

political phenomenon, repeated according to certain rules and within a certain framework. It was the assembly of full citizens, functionally rooted in the constitution of the democracy, an assembly in which fundamental political and judicial decisions were taken... Paul always understands ekklesia as the living, assembled congregation. This is expressed particularly in 1 Cor. 15 (vv. 4f., 12, 19, 23, 28). It is only in the meeting and living together of the members that love, described in 1 Cor. 13 as the supreme gift, can be made real, just as it is only in this way that the other God-given gifts can be recognized and acknowledged."[10]

I think on this level that God is calling his ekklesia to change our language. For example, for years we have said that we are 'going to church'. How are you *going* to church when you *are* the church? When we think about the story of the dry bones we notice that once this army had taken on all of its bodily systems that *they stood an exceeding great army.* Many times we as believers only stand as an army but never carry out orders.

When was the last time you went to a conference, a revival, a concert and received a powerful word that stirred you? In that service, you made vows to the Lord about walking in obedience to Him only to leave and not fulfill what you had vowed. Many of our experiences with God have only been emotional with no fruit.

Have we really had an experience with God?

People who encountered Jesus were never the same. The army in Ezekiel 37 was stuck in a valley; believers are shouting in the valley, dancing in the valley and speaking in tongues in the valley but going nowhere in the realm of the Spirit. In order for an army to make an impact there must be some type of movement. God is calling us OUT of our normal 'church buildings' and holding us accountable to being the church (ekklesia). We only have one problem as the army of the Lord; we are not UNIFIED!

An army moves strategically against its enemy. The Devil has been very successful in keeping us divided; from quarreling amongst ourselves to starting more and more denominations. The spirit of religion has played a big part in keeping us separated. It is sometimes sad to see the world operating together more than the church. There must be a change and we must move as the Spirit leads us.

Prophetically, I see God organizing his army. The Lord revealed a mighty revelation to me one day. In the first century church, we can see from the New Testament that she operated in the power of God. Many souls were saved, healed and delivered. Miracles, signs, and wonders were a common thing for the believer. When people were added to the Kingdom there were real bonafide disciples; The Church was in sync with the movement of the Spirit.

Over time this structure of ministry began to fall apart. Today in the 21st century we see a totally different church. We see a church that has a form of godliness, but denying the power thereof (2 Tim. 3:5). It is rare to see signs, miracles, and wonders following the life of a believer. The Church enjoys being entertained by their favorite preacher or singer. The five-fold ministry gifts are not fully accepted. Millions of saints are content with worshipping together on one day a week while declaring they are doing the work of God.

I see a change happening in the 21st century church. Let me explain. When I was getting the revelation for this book it was the year, 2012. This is what he showed me: When you switch the number 21 around it becomes 12. I believe in the life of the church that God is putting a demand on unity in the body this year. Twelve is a number of apostolic fullness and divine government. If you are an apostle, there should be a mighty stirring in this season in your spirit to bring order and unity to the army of God. 2012 falls in the 21st century. The number two is a number for unity and the number one is a number for compound unity. If you haven't noticed by now that the word 'unity' has appeared twice with both of these numbers. Though years have passed this revelation is still relevant today.

Finally, the number 21 means breakthrough. Once the church gets on one accord in understanding her identity and mission there will be a mighty breakthrough in the realm of the Spirit. We will break through satanic walls of religion. I believe in the 21st Century church that God is taking us back to our roots similar to the first century church. I say similar because I believe that God will do even more through us because of the changing of the times. The 21st Century Church will receive apostolic strategies to advance the Kingdom of God in this end time. I am not sure, but I won't be surprised if Jesus' second coming will happen during this time. I know that is a strong statement but there is such a shift that is happening in the Spirit right now and we must position ourselves for this great move. The Kingdom of God will reign here in this earth realm. To God be the glory!

Small Group Discussion Questions

1. How has this chapter changed your thoughts about the church as you know it?

2. What are your thoughts on the Book of Haggai revelation?

3. What has God shown you for the 21st Century church?

Chapter 9

Prophetic Decrees and Declarations

As we come to a close, I think that it is necessary to release and activate the people of God. As you have read this book, I hope that there was a stirring in you to experience what God has for you in this season of your life. The prophet Ezekiel, in Ezekiel 37, was instructed by God in his vision to prophesy to the dry bones and to prophesy to the wind. To prophesy in this scripture means to bubble up or to pour forth words abundantly. In this chapter I want to prophesy to the dry bones that I see in the Church that she will come alive and be what Christ has called her to be. A movement will start once the army decides to move. Feel free to declare this corporately in your local churches.

Father in the name of Jesus, we/I come as your humble servant(s), your ambassador(s), your mighty warrior(s) thanking you for this time to encounter you. We/I am/are ready to do what you have called me/us to do here in this world. Now by the power of the Holy Ghost, we/I decree and declare over the Body of Christ in this community, city, nation, and region that every system that makes up the body will come alive. We/I speak to the winds of the Spirit to come and breathe in me/us to activate our/my respiratory system so that we/I may come alive. You said that in you we/I live, move and have my being. (Acts 17:28). I/We declare your word that says that man shall not live by bread alone, but by every word that proceeds out of the mouth of God (Mat. 4:4) to be released over our/my digestive system.

Let the vitamins, minerals and nutrients of your word be absorbed in the body for health. I/We release the scripture that says, "Let this mind be in you which was also in Christ Jesus over our/my spiritual nervous system. I/We decree to the skeletal system to be revived to cause the Body of Christ to stand upright in order to withstand and stand against the Kingdom of Darkness. I/We speak divine strength to the muscular system both involuntary and voluntary for proper movement in the things of God. I/We rebuke stagnation NOW in the name of Jesus. Let supernatural strength come into the churches that are struggling and crying out for you Father. Let the endocrine system be stirred to excite and ignite prophetic and apostolic seasons in this time. I/We stir up the immune system so that the body can guard itself against carnality. God awaken callings, giftings, anointings, and mantles in the name of Jesus by the power of the Holy Spirit.

Let the warrior anointings and mantles of David, Joshua, Samson, Gideon, Deborah, Othniel and Ehud rest upon us/me. I/We speak that the Kingdom Warrior arise and be released in education, family, government, media, arts, Church and business to take it for the Kingdom of God. I/We bind the spirit of dissension and loose the spirit of unity and oneness on the Body in this time and season. I/We lose Ephesians 4:4-6 that says, "There is one body, and one Spirit, even as ye are called in one hope of your calling; One Lord, one faith, one baptism, One God and Father of all, who is above all and through all and in you all". I/We lose prophetic and apostolic direction on the Kingdom Warrior to walk in the steps that have been ordered by God.

Let divine wisdom, knowledge, understanding, ideas, thoughts, methodologies, ideologies, philosophies, and concepts be released for the advancement of the Kingdom. Let the angelic hosts be released to retrieve all the spoils and treasures of darkness and secret places to be handed over to the Kingdom Warrior for proper distribution of wealth for the Kingdom NOW. Let waves of the anointing expose the plans and strategies of the enemy. I/We stir up the senses of sight, smell, touch, taste and hearing in the realm of the Spirit to be increased on the Warrior. God we/I thank you for the victory over laziness, procrastination and stagnation. Let the ROAR of God penetrate every kingdom and system of this world for your glory. Jehovah Tesaboath, arise in your people in your Church. According to Psalm 68:1, "Let God arise, let his enemies be scattered..." We thank you Father and we count it done in the matchless name of Jesus Christ amen.

Notes:

1. Brain Center America, Inc, Brain Functions: Visuo-Spatial Skills, 2008, http://www.braincenteramerica.com/visuospa.php

2. R.W. Shambach, A New Anointing for a New Millennium, (15,16)

3. Michelle Miley, How Long Does it Take for Human Bones to Decompose?, 2010, http://www.answerbag.com/q_view/2084250#ixzz1VLqTDhVM- (accessed June 23, 2012)

4. Discovery Kids: Your Endocrine System, 2011, http://kids.discovery.com/tell-me/science/body-systems/your-endocrine-system

5. Mark Cichocki, R.N., The Immune System: Understanding the Parts of Your Immune System, 2009, http://aids.about.com/od/drugfactsheets/a/immuneseries.htm

6. Pastor Jack Thoemke, The Simple Gospel Beauty of Holiness, www.pointing2jesus.com (accessed June 23, 2012)

7. Healthwise Staff, Alcohol Effects on a Fetus Causes, Symptoms and Treatment, 2011, http://www.revolutionhealth.com/healthy-living/pregnancy/the-effects-of-alcohol-on-an-unborn-baby

8. Dr. Cindy Trimm, The Rules of Engagement: The Art of Strategic Prayer and Spiritual Warfare, (pg. 186, 187)

9. Andy Zoppelt, Origin of the Word "church" Part 1: The Word that Changed the World, 2006 , www.therealchurch.com

10. The History of the Word "CHURCH", http://www.aotfb.com/ekklesia/church.html

An apostolic and prophetic ministry with a divine mandate to restore the Church back to its biblical foundations as it advances the Kingdom of God within the seven spheres (mountains) of society: Government, Media, Marketplace, Arts & Entertainment, Education, Family and the Church

FOR MORE INFORMATION PLEASE VISIT OUR SITE

www.warcriersministries.weebly.com

A coaching, training & development and consulting organization that was established to provide services to inspiring individuals who are looking to be the catalyst for change in the world for the 21st century. We develop the next generational leaders through cutting edge trainings, workshops, seminars and consultation from a Kingdom perspective. Our goal is to undergird educational institutions in order to provide students with the necessary tools that will help to cultivate purpose, leadership skills and life skills. We want to see the next generation initiating movements within the seven spheres of society (Education, Government, Arts & Entertainment, Religion, Media, Family, Marketplace)

FOR MORE INFORMATION PLEASE VISIT OUR SITE

www.roarinstitute.weebly.com

REGULAR EVENTS FOR OUR MINISTRY:

THE WARRIOR'S CHAMBER

Do you want to know what God is doing with his Church now? Are you hungry for the meat of the Word? Do you feel like a sheep just wandering? We welcome you to worship with our home church atmosphere every Friday evening at 7pm. YOU WILL NOT LEAVE THE SAME!!

THE ELIJAH COMPANY

Join us every last Friday of the month for a prophetic training environment for those that want to be activated and cultivated in the prophetic ministry.

THE SUMMIT PRAYER GATHERING: REPAIRING THE CITY ALTAR

Join us once a month for our corporate city wide prayer gathering held every first Friday night. If you are looking for the glory to manifest in your city then you don't want to miss this unified war cry to the heavens.

"THE ENCOUNTER" WORSHIP SERVICE

Join us once a month for a unified city wide worship gathering to hear the word of the Lord for our city.

www.ingramcontent.com/pod-product-compliance
Lightning Source LLC
Chambersburg PA
CBHW071314110426
42743CB00042B/1786